Homework Book

Series Editor
Paul Metcalf

Series Advisor
David Hodgson

Lead Author
Steven Lomax

June Haighton
Anne Haworth
Janice Johns
Andrew Manning
Kathryn Scott
Chris Sherrington
Margaret Thornton
Mark Willis

HIGHER
Linear 1

2nd edition

Nelson Thornes
a Wolters Kluwer business

Published in 2006 by:
Nelson Thornes Ltd
Delta Place
27 Bath Road
CHELTENHAM
GL53 7TH
United Kingdom

07 08 09 10 / 10 9 8 7 6 5 4 3

A catalogue record for this book is available from the British Library.

ISBN 978 0 7487 8209 3

Cover photograph: Salmon by Kyle Krause/Index Stock/OSF/Photolibrary
Page make-up by MCS Publishing Services Ltd, Salisbury, Wiltshire

Printed and bound in Spain by GraphyCems

Acknowledgements

The authors and publishers wish to thank the following for their contribution:
David Bowles for providing the Assess questions
David Hodgson for reviewing draft manuscripts

Thank you to the following schools:
Little Heath School, Reading
The Kingswinford School, Dudley
Thorne Grammar School, Doncaster

The publishers thank the following for permission to reproduce copyright material:

Vitruvian Man – Corel 481 (NT): p. 113

The publishers have made every effort to contact copyright holders but apologise if any have been overlooked.

Contents

Introduction

This book contains homework that allows you to practise what
you have just learned. Each chapter is divided into sections that
correspond to the numbered Learn topics for the matching
chapter in the Students' Book.

 Means that these questions should be attempted with a calculator.

 Means that these questions are practice for the non-calculator
paper in the exam and should be attempted without a calculator.

1 ◄——————— Underlined questions are harder questions.

1 Statistical measures

Homework 1

1 Write down the time you spend on each of these activities each week.

   a sleeping   **b** homework   **c** watching television

   Calculate the mean numbers of hours for each and write your answers to the nearest hour.

2 In a survey on the number of people in a household the following information was collected from 50 houses.

Number of people in a household	Number of households
1	9
2	19
3	9
4	8
5	4
6	1
Total	50

   a Find the mean, median, mode and range of household sizes.

   b Which average is the best one to use to represent the data? Explain your answer.

3 The graph shows the frequency of goals scored by a football team during a season.

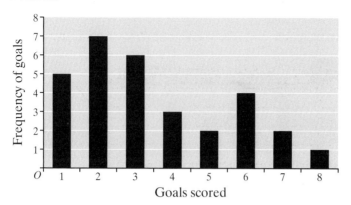

Goals scored

a How many matches were played during the season?

b What is the modal score?

c What is the median number of goals scored?

d What is the mean score?

e What is the range of the number of goals scored?

4 Miss Saunders divided her class of 40 students into two groups, A and B. She gave each group the same test which was marked out of 10. The results are shown in the table below.

Number of marks	0	1	2	3	4	5	6	7	8	9	10
Group A frequency	3	0	0	5	1	6	1	2	0	0	0
Group B frequency	0	0	0	3	3	3	6	4	1	1	1

Which group did better?
Compare the two groups by finding the range and mean scores.

5 This bar chart shows the number of letters in words in a crossword puzzle.

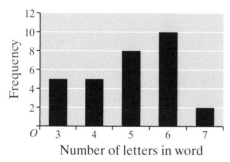

Number of letters in word

Find the

a median   **b** mode   **c** mean   **d** range of the number of letters.

e Which average best represents the distribution?
Give a reason for your answer.

Homework 2

1   This table gives the number of years' service by 50 teachers at the Clare School.

Number of years' service	Number of teachers
0–4	11
5–9	15
10–14	4
15–19	10
20–24	6
25–30	4

   a Find the modal class.

   b Calculate an estimate of the mean.

2   In a science lesson, 30 runner bean plants were measured. Here are the results correct to the nearest centimetre.

6.2	5.4	8.9	12.1	6.5	9.3	7.2	12.7	10.2	5.4
7.7	9.5	11.1	8.6	7.0	13.5	12.7	5.6	15.4	12.3
13.4	9.5	6.7	8.6	9.1	11.5	14.2	13.5	8.8	9.7

The teacher suggested that the data was put into groups.

Length in centimetres	Tally	Total
5 but less than 7		
7 but less than 9		
9 but less than 11		
11 but less than 13		
13 but less than 15		
15 but less than 17		

   a Copy and complete the table.

   b Use the information to work out an estimate of the mean height of the plants.

   c Calculate the mean from the original data.

   d Why is your answer to part **b** only an estimate of the mean?

3 The heights of 50 students at Eastham School were measured.
The results were put into a table.

Height (h cm)	Frequency
$149.5 \leqslant h < 154.5$	4
$154.5 \leqslant h < 159.5$	21
$159.5 \leqslant h < 164.5$	18
$164.5 \leqslant h < 169.5$	7

Estimate the mean value of the distribution.

2 Integers

1 Write all the factors of these numbers.

    a 16   **b** 24   **c** 60   **d** 100

2 Write the first five multiples of these numbers.

    a 4   **b** 10   **c** 14

3 Find the least common multiple (LCM) of each set of numbers.

    a 2 and 7   **c** 4 and 5   **e** 4, 6 and 9

    b 5 and 3   **d** 8 and 5

4 Find the highest common factor (HCF) of each set of numbers.

    a 8 and 12   **c** 12 and 18   **e** 48 and 72

    b 8 and 18   **d** 24 and 30

5 Look at these numbers:

    2, 3, 4, 5, 6, 7, 8, 9, 10, 11, 12, 13, 14, 15

    a Which are factors of 12?

    b Which are multiples of 6?

    c Which are factors of 15?

    d Which are multiples of 4?

6 **Get Real!**

Two buses stop at the same bus stop.
On one route the bus stops every 25 minutes.
On the other route the bus stops every 40 minutes.
If both buses leave the stop at 9 a.m., at what time should the buses next reach the stop together?

7 One light flashes every 8 seconds.
A second light flashes every 10 seconds and a third every 15 seconds.
If the three lights start flashing at the same time, after how long will they flash together again?

8 In a 10 000 m race, one runner is taking 64 seconds a lap.
Another runner takes 72 seconds a lap.
After how many laps will the faster runner first lap the slower runner?

Homework 2

1 Write the following numbers as products of prime factors.

    a 52   **b** 60   **c** 44   **d** 64   **e** 80

2 Express each number as a product of its prime factors.
Write your answers using index notation.

    a 70   **b** 96   **c** 100   **d** 150   **e** 256

3 Write 126 as a product of prime factors.

4 p and q are prime numbers. Find the values of p and q when $p^3 \times q = 24$.

5 What numbers are these?

    a It is a prime number. It is a factor of 91. It is not a factor of 26.

    b It is a prime number. It is a factor of 132. It is bigger than 5.

6 Look at this set of numbers.

    8   37   73   91   180   270   360

    a Which two numbers are prime numbers?

    b Which number can be written in index form as $2^3 \times 3^2 \times 5$?

7 What are the prime factors of 1000?
Write your answer using index notation.

8 A number expressed as a product of its prime factors is $2^6 \times 3^4 \times 5^2$.
What is the number?

9 Express these numbers in prime factors and find their
(**i**) highest common factor (HCF) and (**ii**) least common multiple (LCM)

    a 28, 16   **b** 64, 24   **c** 80, 48

Homework 3

Apart from question 6, this is a non-calculator exercise.

1 Find the reciprocal of these numbers.

   a 2   **b** 9   **c** 6   **d** 15

2 Find the reciprocal of these numbers.

   a $\frac{1}{3}$ **b** $\frac{1}{14}$ **c** $\frac{1}{11}$ **d** $\frac{2}{5}$

3 What is the value of $1 \div \frac{1}{4}$?

4 Find the reciprocal of these numbers.

   a 0.2   **b** 0.75   **c** 0.6   **d** $0.\dot{6}$

5 Find the reciprocal of these numbers.

   a $3\frac{1}{5}$ **b** $6\frac{7}{8}$ **c** $2\frac{3}{5}$ **d** $4\frac{9}{10}$

<u>6</u> Find the reciprocals of the numbers from 30 to 40.
Write them to 4 decimal places if they are not exact decimals.
Which of the numbers have reciprocals that are:

   a exact decimals

   b decimals with one recurring figure

   c decimals with two recurring figures

   d decimals with three recurring figures?

3 Rounding

Do not use your calculator for estimating!
You may, though, want to check your answers with the help of your calculator.

1 For each question, decide which estimate is best.

		Estimate A	Estimate B	Estimate C
a	3.67 × 7.4	2.8	2.1	28
b	1.8 × 21.4	4	40	400
c	12.34 ÷ 4.1	3	0.3	48
d	51.5 × 9.8	5	50	500
e	6.1 ÷ 2.1	0.3	3	30
f	44.1 × 1.8	80	44	440
g	6.8 ÷ 1.1	7	70	0.7
h	2.8 × 4.2 ÷ 3.8	3	2	1
i	31.9 ÷ 6.2 × 3.2	2	150	15

2 For each pair of calculations, estimate the answers to help you decide which you think will have the larger answer.

a 4.2×2.8 or 5.1×2.3

b $33.3 \div 6.2$ or 2.31×2.78

c $13.41 - 4.28$ or $27.5 \div 2.14$

d 59.4×31.6 or 95.3×9.8

3 Estimate the answers to these calculations by rounding to one significant figure.

a $8.6 + 4.9$

b $7.9 \div 2.1$

c $59.1 + 40.8$

d 9.1×8.8

e 0.2×6

f $\dfrac{52.1 \times 4.7}{4.8}$

g $\dfrac{33.7 + 53.2}{77.1 - 68.5}$

h $\dfrac{3.6 \times 7.1}{0.11}$

i $\dfrac{89.8 \times 5.9}{0.32}$

j $23.9(5.35 + 2.79)$

k $\dfrac{38.2 \times 7.9}{0.48}$

l $\dfrac{89.8 + 5.9}{0.32}$

m $23.9(5.35 - 2.79)$

4 **a** Write down two consecutive whole numbers, one that is smaller than the square root of 40 and one that is larger.

  b Write down two consecutive whole numbers, one that is smaller than the square root of 120 and one that is larger.

5 Estimate 6.32 + 4.26 by rounding to the nearest whole number.

  Explain why the answer is an underestimate of the exact answer.

6 A group of 29 people weigh a total of 2772 kg.

  Estimate their mean weight.

  Is this a reasonable amount for the mean weight of a large number of people?

7 Estimate the total cost of 58 computers at £885 each.

8 Estimate the square roots of these numbers.

  a 15   **b** 30   **c** 60   **d** 5   **e** 2000

9 Estimate 4.13 × 8.22 by rounding to one significant figure.

  Explain why the answer is an underestimate of the exact answer.

10 Joe estimated the answer to 12.2 ÷ 8.2 as 1.5 by rounding both numbers down. Does this mean that 1.5 is an underestimate of the correct answer?

11 Explain why 2.4 ÷ 0.6 has the same answer as 24 ÷ 6 and 240 ÷ 60.

12 Which of these make a number larger and which of them make it smaller?

  a Dividing by 10   **c** Dividing by 0.1
  b Multiplying by 10   **d** Multiplying by 0.1

13 Estimate the answers to:

  a 41 ÷ 8.2   **b** 41 ÷ 0.82   **c** 41 ÷ 0.082

14 **a** Find five numbers whose square roots are between 9 and 10.

  b Find two consecutive whole numbers to complete this statement:

    'The square root of 70 is between ... and ... '

15 **Get Real!**
  Estimate the total cost of five CDs costing £6.98 each.

16 Estimate how many bottles of water costing 47 pence each you can buy for £8.

17 Estimate how much fencing is needed for a rectangular field measuring 48.5 m by 63 m.

18 A group of nine people wins £4855 on the lottery.
Estimate how much each person will get when the money is shared out equally.

19 Matt drives at an average speed of 57.8 miles an hour for 2 hours 55 minutes.
Estimate how far he goes.

Homework 2

1 Each of these quantities is rounded to the nearest whole number of units. Write down the minimum and maximum possible size of each quantity.

a 26 g	**c** 225 m	**e** 33 kg
b 4 cm	**d** 13 litres	**f** £249

2 The upper bound of a length measured to three significant figures is 3.295 m.

If the actual length is x metres, copy and complete this statement:
$... \leqslant x < ...$.

3 Get Real!
A man is allowed to carry loads up to a total of 25 kg. He is asked to carry 12 packets weighing 2 kg each, measured correct to the nearest 100 g. Can he complain about this? Explain your reasoning.

4 The amount of breakfast cereal in a packet is designed to be 510 g with an acceptable limit of 2 per cent either way. What is the minimum possible weight of cereal in the packet?

5 The weight of a toffee is 5 g correct to the nearest half gram. What is the minimum possible weight of 100 of these toffees?

4 Use of symbols

1 Multiply out the following.

    a $2(x + 3)$ **e** $3(d - 4)$ **i** $8(g - 2) + 4(g + 2)$

    b $4(y + 4)$ **f** $5(3ab + 2a)$ **j** $7(h + 2) + 3(2 - h)$

    c $2(t + 1)$ **g** $-2(x + 1)$ **k** $3(2 - a) - 4(a - 2)$

    d $6(h - 2)$ **h** $-3(p - 2)$

2 Expand:

    a $p(p + 2)$ **e** $w(2w - 3)$ **i** $2a(a + 1) + 4a(3 + a)$

    b $y(y + 4)$ **f** $2k(3k + 4)$ **j** $3x(y + 2) + 2y(x - 1)$

    c $b(2b + 3)$ **g** $5t(3t - 4)$ **k** $\dfrac{y}{3}(6y - 1) + \dfrac{y}{6}(4 + 3y)$

    d $g(g - 4)$ **h** $4a(2b - 3)$

3 Expand:

    a $p^2(p^2 + 4)$ **d** $w^3(w^2 - 3)$ **g** $3x^2y(2xy - 4xy^2)$

    b $d^3(d^2 + 5)$ **e** $2a(3a^2 + 5)$ **h** $\dfrac{a}{2}(6ab - 2a)$

    c $t^2(t^5 - 3)$ **f** $4p(4p - 3pq)$ **i** $3xy^2z(2xz + 3yz)$

1 Expand and simplify:

    a $(x + 4)(x + 2)$ **d** $(f - 2)(f - 6)$ **g** $(3y + 2)(2y - 3)$

    b $(p + 3)(p + 4)$ **e** $(x + 2)^2$

    c $(d - 2)(d + 5)$ **f** $(2x + 3)(x - 2)$

2 The answer is $x^2 - 2x + c$ where c is an integer. Find five expressions in the form $(x + a)(x + b)$ with this answer, stating the values of a, b and c each time.

3 Expand and simplify:

a $(2x + y)(x + 3y)$ **e** $(3x - y)(x - 2y)$ **i** $(3x + 2y)^2$

b $(3p + q)(3p + 2q)$ **f** $(2x - 4)(2x + 4)$ **j** $(5p - 2q)^2$

c $(3a - b)(2a + b)$ **g** $(6t - 2s)(3t - 4s)$

d $(4p + 2q)(3p - 2q)$ **h** $(a + b)^2$

Homework 3

1 Factorise:

a $5ab + 2b$ **e** $11ab - 7bc$ **i** $2p^2q + 5pq^2$

b $4pq + q$ **f** $p^2 + 3p$ **j** $3x^2yz^3 + 6xy^2z - 12xyz$

c $7ty + 10y$ **g** $2x^2 + xy$

d $3xz + 5x^2z$ **h** $4p^2 + 6pq$

2 Match the expression with the correct factorisation.
Fill in the missing expressions and factorisations.

Expression	Factorisation
$d^2 + 5d$	$2(5a - 8)$
	$5(d + 1)$
$3p^2q + 12pq^2$	
$10a - 16$	
	$4p^2q(q + 3)$

3 Factorise:

a $2x + 2y + x^2 + xy$ **c** $10p + 2q + 15p + 3q$ **e** $4(x + y)^2 + 3(x + y)$

b $ab + 3a + 2b + 6$ **d** $8d + 4 - 2d^2 - d$

Homework 4

1 Factorise:

a $y^2 + 7y + 6$ **e** $b^2 + 2b - 3$ **i** $x^2 - 36$

b $t^2 + t - 6$ **f** $x^2 + 4x - 32$ **j** $k^2 - 121$

c $p^2 - 5p - 6$ **g** $x^2 + 10x - 24$ **k** $x^2 - a^2$

d $x^2 - 10x + 9$ **h** $p^2 + 10d + 7$ **l** $8 - 2x - x^2$

HINT
One of these expressions cannot be factorised.

2 Factorise:

   a $2x^2 + 10x + 12$ **d** $7x^2 - 62x + 48$ **g** $a^2 - 16b^2$

   b $3x^2 + 7x + 2$ **e** $4x^2 + 14x + 6$ **h** $2a^2 - 18b^2$

   c $3x^2 + 3x - 6$ **f** $6x^2 - 10x - 4$

Homework 5

1 Simplify these expressions.

   a $\dfrac{x^2 + 5x}{x + 5}$ **c** $\dfrac{x^2 + 8x + 7}{x + 1}$ **e** $\dfrac{x^2 + 4x - 5}{x^2 + 2x - 15}$

   b $\dfrac{x^2 + 6x + 8}{x + 4}$ **d** $\dfrac{2(x - 2)^2}{(x - 2)}$

2 Simplify these expressions.

   a $\dfrac{3x^2 + 5x + 2}{x + 1}$ **d** $\dfrac{x^2 + 2x}{x^2 - 4}$ **g** $\dfrac{5x^2 + 9x - 2}{2x^2 - 8}$

   b $\dfrac{2x^2 + 7x + 6}{2x + 3}$ **e** $\dfrac{2x^2 - x - 6}{3x^2 - 5x - 2}$

   c $\dfrac{x^2 - 9}{x + 3}$ **f** $\dfrac{3x^2 - x - 10}{9x^2 - 25}$

5 Decimals

1 Work out:

   a 3.2×3.2 **c** 3.2×0.52 **e** 4.6×7.8 **g** 0.67×0.43

   b 4.2×1.4 **d** 4.2×9.1 **f** 5.6×3.4 **h** 0.345×0.03

2 Using your answers to question **1**, write down the answers to these multiplications.

   a 3.2×0.32 **c** 32×0.52 **e** 4.6×0.078 **g** 67×0.43

   b 4.2×0.14 **d** 0.42×0.91 **f** 0.0056×3.4 **h** 34.5×30

3 Neeta knows $4 \times 7 = 28$. She says that $0.4 \times 0.7 = 0.28$

   Joe says $0.4 \times 0.7 = 2.8$

   Who is right? Explain your answer.

4 You can split 8 into two parts, 2 and 6. Then multiply: $2 \times 6 = 12$

   You can split 8 into two parts, 3 and 5. Then multiply: $3 \times 5 = 15$

   Split 8 into two parts and multiply them together. Your aim is to get close to 14. How close can you get? (You will need to use decimals.)

5 A palindrome reads the same forwards as backwards.

   So 4.2×2.4 is a palindrome. So is 1.5×5.1

   a Which is bigger, 4.2×2.4 or 1.5×5.1?

   b Which is bigger, 6.2×2.6 or 3.5×5.3?

   c Which is bigger, 9.2×2.9 or 7.4×4.7?

   In parts **a–c**, the two numbers have the same sum.

   For example, in part **a**, $4.2 + 2.4 = 1.5 + 5.1$

   d Here are two more. Can you predict which will have the bigger answer before you work them out?

     i 7.2×2.7 or 4.5×5.4

     ii 5.7×7.5 or 3.9×9.3

   e Can you find any multiplications with a palindromic answer, for example, $3.3 \times 3.7 = 12.21$?

Homework 2

1 Work out $414 \div 6$

2 Use your answer to question **1** to work these out:

    a $41.4 \div 6$ **b** $4.14 \div 0.6$ **c** $0.414 \div 0.06$ **d** $414 \div 0.6$

3 Eight friends go out for a meal. The total cost is £100.32
They decide to split the cost equally between them.

    How much should they each pay?

4 Work out:

    a $2.45 \div 0.5$ **c** $2.34 \div 0.8$ **e** $9.65 \div 0.5$ **g** $8.765 \div 0.1$

    b $9.12 \div 0.6$ **d** $9.6 \div 0.12$ **f** $24.97 \div 1.1$ **h** $0.005 \div 0.4$

5 Get Real!

The Healthy Bite Café buys orange juice in big containers. Each container holds 15 litres of juice.

    a How many 0.3 litre cups can they get from a 15 litre container?

    b If they charge £0.85 for each cup, how much money do they get from all these cups?

    c They pay £23.85 for a big container. How much profit do they make?

6 Get Real!

Aisha goes to the supermarket and sees some bottles of squash on offer at £1.10 each. She has £30 in her pocket.

    a How many bottles can she buy?

    b Work out the exact cost of these bottles.

    c How much change will she have left?

7 Work out:

    a $4.96 \div 1.6$ **c** $0.51 \div 1.5$ **e** $7.263 \div 1.8$

    b $7.222 \div 2.3$ **d** $21.06 \div 2.6$ **f** $0.02 \div 400$

8 If $2.6 \times 3.3 = 8.58$, write down the answer to:

    a $8.58 \div 0.33$ **b** $85.8 \div 26$ **c** $0.858 \div 26$ **d** $85.8 \div 0.033$

Homework 3 🔲

Apart from question 7, this is a non-calculator exercise.

1 Change these decimals to fractions.

 a 0.7 **b** 0.35 **c** 0.85 **d** 0.26 **e** 0.375 **f** 0.325

2 Change these fractions to decimals.

 a $\frac{2}{5}$ **b** $\frac{3}{10}$ **c** $\frac{7}{20}$ **d** $\frac{5}{8}$

3 Change these fractions to recurring decimals.

 a $\frac{2}{3}$ **b** $\frac{5}{6}$ **c** $\frac{2}{7}$ **d** $\frac{5}{12}$

4 James thinks 0.38 is the same as $\frac{3}{8}$

 a Is James correct?
 Give a reason for your answer.

 b Which is bigger, 0.38 or $\frac{3}{8}$?

 c How much bigger? Give your answer as a fraction and a decimal.

5 **a** Change 0.5 and 0.05 to fractions.

 b Now change 0.6 and 0.06 to fractions.

 c What do you notice?

 d If $0.65 = \frac{13}{20}$, what decimal do you think is equal to $\frac{13}{200}$?

6 If $\frac{3}{8} = 0.375$, what is the decimal equivalent of

 a $\frac{3}{80}$ **b** $\frac{6}{80}$ **c** $\frac{3}{16}$?

7 **a** Use a calculator to change these fractions to decimals.

 i $\frac{1}{9}$ **ii** $\frac{12}{99}$ **iii** $\frac{123}{999}$

 b There is a pattern in the questions, and a pattern in the answers.
 Use the patterns to predict a fraction which is equal to
 0.12345123451234512345 ...

 Check you are right by changing your answer to a decimal.

Homework 4

 1 Write the following recurring decimals as fractions.

   a $0.\dot{1}$ **b** $0.\dot{1}\dot{2}$ **c** $0.\dot{1}2\dot{3}$

 2 Change these fractions into recurring decimals.

   a $\frac{5}{11}$ **b** $\frac{7}{111}$

 3 Find a fraction that is equal to:

   a $0.\dot{3}\dot{6}$ **b** $0.3\dot{6}$

 4 Barry says that $\frac{4}{7} = 0.571428\dot{}$

   Harry says that $\frac{4}{7} = 0.\dot{5}71428\dot{}$

   Larry says that $\frac{4}{7} = 0.\dot{5}71428\dot{5}$

   Who is right?

   Give a reason for your answer.

 5 It is easy to find decimals with one recurring digit, or two recurring digits. What other numbers of recurring digits can you find, and what fractions lead to them?

 6 The Fibonnaci sequence starts 1, 1, 2, 3, 5, 8, 13, ...

   a Key this sequence into your calculator:

      $1 \times 10 = \times 10 + 1 \times 10 = \times 10 + 2 \times 10 = \times 10 + 3 \times 10 = ...$

      These numbers are the Fibonacci sequence.

      Write down the display each time you press the [=] key.

   b Work out the recurring decimal for $\frac{1}{89}$

   c What do you notice about your answers?

6 Area and volume

Homework 1

1 Find the area of each of these triangles.

a

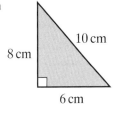

10 cm
8 cm
6 cm

Not drawn accurately

c

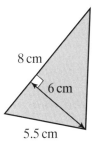

8 cm
6 cm
5.5 cm

b

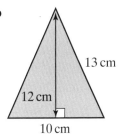

13 cm
12 cm
10 cm

d

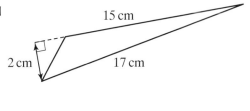

15 cm
2 cm
17 cm

2 Find the area of each of these parallelograms.

a

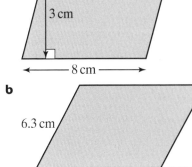

3 cm
8 cm

b

6.3 cm
6 cm
10 cm

c

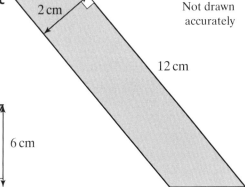

2 cm
Not drawn accurately
12 cm
5 cm

3 Fill in the gaps in the table.

	Shape (Parallelogram/Triangle)	Base	Perpendicular height	Area
a	Parallelogram	5 cm	2.5 cm	
b	Triangle	5 cm	18 cm	
c		10 cm	2.5 cm	12.5 cm²
d	Parallelogram	4 cm		12 cm²
e	Triangle	0.5 cm		8 cm²
f	Parallelogram	0.5 m	10 cm	

Homework 2

1 Estimate the area of the island where each square represents one square mile.

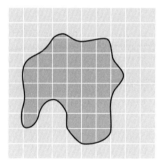

2 **a** Find the area of each of the following shapes made from 1 cm squares.

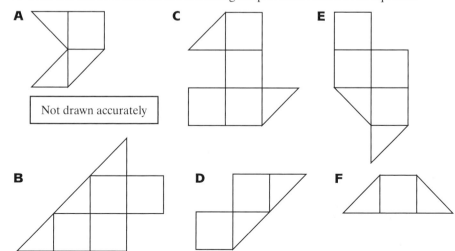

A

C

E

Not drawn accurately

B

D

F

b Draw a shape with an area of $5\frac{1}{2}$ cm².

3 Calculate the shaded area in each of the following:

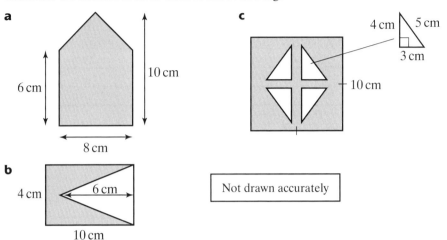

a

6 cm

10 cm

8 cm

c

4 cm   5 cm

3 cm

10 cm

b

4 cm

6 cm

10 cm

Not drawn accurately

4 Find the area of the following shapes:

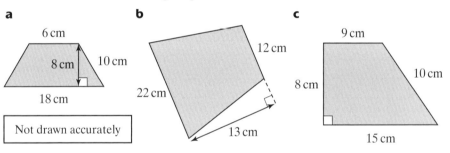

a

6 cm

8 cm   10 cm

18 cm

Not drawn accurately

b

12 cm

22 cm

13 cm

c

9 cm

8 cm

10 cm

15 cm

Homework 3

1 Calculate the circumference of each circle:

a leaving your answer in terms of π

b giving your answer to an appropriate degree of accuracy.

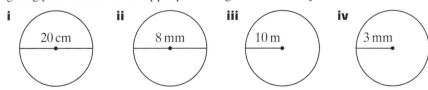

i

20 cm

ii

8 mm

iii

10 m

iv

3 mm

2 Calculate the perimeter of each shape:

 a leaving your answer in terms of π

    b giving your answer to an appropriate degree of accuracy.

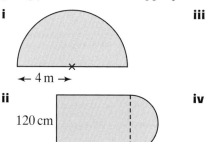

i

← 4 m →

iii

4 mm

ii

120 cm

←— 2 m —→

iv

60°

6 cm

3 Copy and complete this table, giving your answers to an appropriate degree of accuracy.

Radius	Diameter	Circumference
	8 cm	
8 m		
		19.6 mm
		12π cm

4 Calculate the curved surface area of this cylinder.

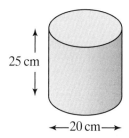

25 cm

←—20 cm—→

5 Find the area of each of these kites.

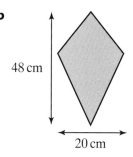

a

10 cm

30 cm

10 cm

b

48 cm

20 cm

Homework 4

1 Calculate the areas of these circles:

 a leaving your answer in terms of π

   b giving your answer to an appropriate degree of accuracy.

i 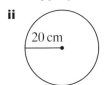 7 cm   **ii** 20 cm   **iii** 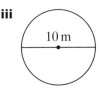 10 m   **iv** 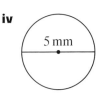 5 mm

2 Copy and complete this table, giving your answers to an appropriate degree of accuracy.

Radius	Diameter	Area
	8 cm	
8 m		
		19.6 mm²
		36π cm²

3 Calculate the total area of each shape:

 a leaving your answer in terms of π

   b giving your answer to an appropriate degree of accuracy.

i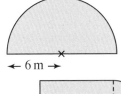
← 6 m →

iii
8 cm

ii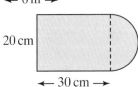
20 cm
← 30 cm →

iv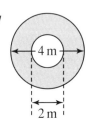
4 m
2 m

4 Calculate the volume of this cylinder.

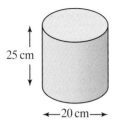

25 cm

←20 cm→

Homework 5

1 Calculate the volumes of these solids, leaving your answer in terms of π where appropriate.

a

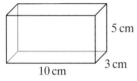

5 cm

3 cm

10 cm

e

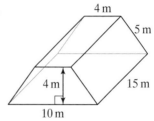

4 m

5 m

4 m

15 m

10 m

b

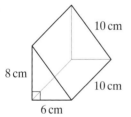

10 cm

8 cm

10 cm

6 cm

f

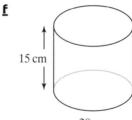

15 cm

← 20 cm →

c

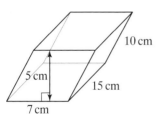

10 cm

5 cm

15 cm

7 cm

g

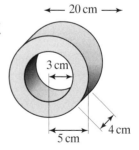

3 cm

5 cm

4 cm

d

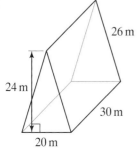

26 m

24 m

30 m

20 m

23

2 Find three different solids with a volume of 120 cm^3.

3 Get Real!

Maximus the Millionaire Mathematician (or M^3 to his friends!) will only play games with his personalised gold dice.

He has a million gold bars like this one.

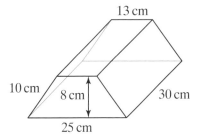
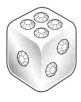

a How many dice (side 3 cm) can he make by melting down one of them?

b If the density of gold is 19.3 g/cm^3, what is the weight of each dice?

4 Copy and complete the table

Solid	Base	Perpendicular height	Length	Volume
	4 cm	2 cm		24 cm^3
	10 cm	5 cm	10 cm	
	5 cm		8 cm	80 cm^3
	Diameter =	N/A	5 cm	80π cm^3

5 Get Real!

The school swimming pool is filled at a rate of 400 litres/min. How long will it take, in hours, to fill up the pool? The dimensions of the pool are shown in the diagram.

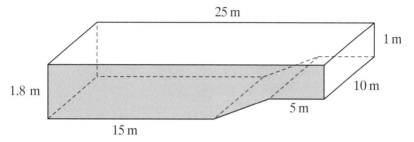

Homework 6

1 **a** Calculate the surface areas of these prisms.

Not drawn accurately

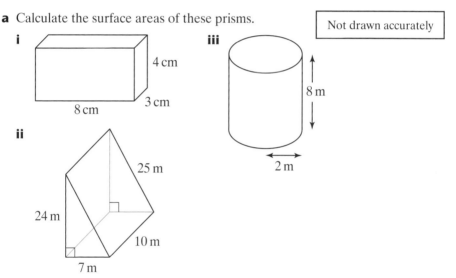

b Convert your answers to parts **ii** and **iii** into cm^2, correct to 3 s.f.

2 **a** Five special solids whose faces are all the same regular polygon are named after the Greek mathematician Plato – they are known as the **Platonic solids**. In the diagrams below, each face has an area of 20 cm^2. Calculate the surface area of each solid.

i   **ii**   **iii**   **iv**   **v**

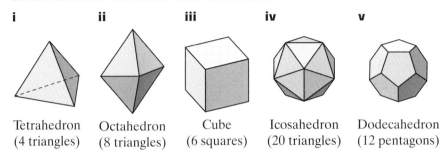

Tetrahedron   Octahedron   Cube   Icosahedron   Dodecahedron
(4 triangles)   (8 triangles) (6 squares) (20 triangles) (12 pentagons)

b Using the internet, find a net for each Platonic solid.

For questions **3** to **7**, match the solid with the correct name, surface area and volume from the table below. All calculations must be shown.

Name	Surface area	Volume
Triangular-based prism	119 cm^2	60 cm^3
Cylinder	150 cm^2	30 cm^3
Pentagonal-based prism	112 cm^2	100 cm^3
Cube	148 cm^2	120 cm^3
Cuboid	76.8 cm^2	125 cm^3

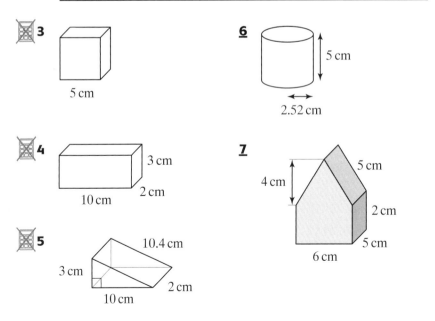

3 5 cm

6 5 cm
2.52 cm

4 3 cm
2 cm
10 cm

7 5 cm
4 cm
2 cm
5 cm
6 cm

5 10.4 cm
3 cm
2 cm
10 cm

Homework 7

1 Find:

   a the volume

   b the total surface area of these solids, giving your answers to a reasonable degree of accuracy.

   i
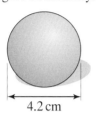
4.2 cm

   iii
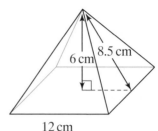
6 cm 8.5 cm
12 cm

   ii
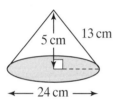
5 cm 13 cm
← 24 cm →

   iv
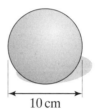
10 cm

2 **Get Real!**

   John has some spherical sweets in a cylindrical pack. He decides to work out the maximum number of sweets in the packet.

   a What is the volume of one sweet?

   b What is the volume of the pack?

   c What is the maximum number of sweets in the pack?

   d How long would the pack have to be to fit one thousand sweets?

   e How long would the pack have to be to fit one million sweets?

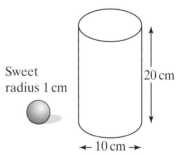

Sweet radius 1 cm

20 cm

← 10 cm →

3 **Get Real!**

   Four juggling balls can fit in the container shown. The radius of one juggling ball is 4 cm. Calculate the amount of volume wasted in the container, leaving your answer in terms of π.

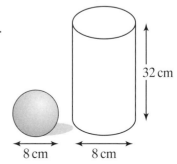

32 cm

8 cm 8 cm

4 Find the volumes of these solids.

a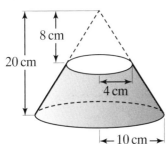

b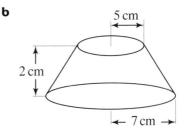

Homework 8

1 **a** Calculate the areas of the shaded sectors, leaving your answer in terms of π.

i

ii

iii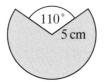

    b Calculate the perimeter of each shape, leaving your answer in terms of π.

2 Calculate the area of the shaded region in each diagram, giving your answer to an appropriate degree of accuracy.

a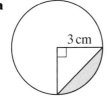

b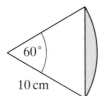

3 Find the length of the *major* arc of a circle with radius: $r = 15$ cm and angle 255°.

4 Find the area of the *major* sector with radius: $r = 15$ cm and angle 255°.

7 Fractions

Homework 1

*You should be able to do all of these without a calculator but make sure you know
how to use a calculator to check your work or to speed it up.*

1 Work out:

a $\frac{3}{10} + \frac{2}{15}$ **b** $\frac{3}{10} - \frac{2}{15}$ **c** $\frac{4}{5} + \frac{3}{8}$ **d** $\frac{4}{5} - \frac{3}{8}$

2 Work out:

a $2\frac{3}{10} + 1\frac{2}{15}$ **b** $2\frac{3}{10} - 1\frac{2}{15}$ **c** $3\frac{1}{4} + 1\frac{1}{3}$ **d** $3\frac{1}{3} - 1\frac{1}{4}$

3 Work out:

a $2\frac{2}{15} + 1\frac{3}{10}$ **b** $2\frac{2}{15} - 1\frac{3}{10}$ **c** $3\frac{1}{3} + 1\frac{1}{4}$ **d** $4\frac{1}{4} - 1\frac{2}{3}$

4 How many times does $\frac{2}{3}$ go into 4? (Work this out by repeatedly
subtracting $\frac{2}{3}$ from 4.)

5 Find the sum of $1\frac{2}{3}$ and $2\frac{1}{5}$

6 **a** John says, 'When you double $2\frac{1}{2}$ you get $4\frac{1}{4}$.'
Is John right? Show how you worked out your answer.

    b Lynn says, '$\frac{4}{5}$ plus $\frac{1}{3}$ is $\frac{5}{8}$.'
Is Lynn right? Show how you worked out your answer.

7 Without working out the answers, arrange these calculations in order,
the one with the smallest answer first and the one with the largest
answer last.

$1 + \frac{2}{3}$ $1 - \frac{2}{3}$ $1 + \frac{4}{3}$ $1 - \frac{4}{3}$

8 Find three different pairs of fractions that add up to 6.

9 **Get Real!**
David's recipe says that he needs two thirds of a cup of cream for some
ice cream for four people. How much cream does he need if he wants to
make ice cream for eight people?

10 Get Real!

Diane is making hats and bags for a school sale.

Each hat needs $\frac{3}{8}$ of a yard of fabric and each bag needs $\frac{2}{3}$ of a yard.

How much fabric is needed to make a hat and bag set?

Homework 2

1 Work out:

a $15 \times \frac{1}{5}$ **c** $36 \times \frac{2}{3}$ **e** $15 \times \frac{4}{5}$ **g** $36 \times \frac{5}{9}$

b $26 \times \frac{1}{2}$ **d** $45 \times \frac{2}{9}$ **f** $26 \times \frac{1}{4}$ **h** $45 \times \frac{3}{10}$

2 Work out:

a $\frac{4}{5} \times \frac{1}{2}$ **c** $\frac{3}{4} \times \frac{1}{3}$ **e** $\frac{7}{9} \times \frac{3}{7}$ **g** $\frac{2}{3} \times \frac{5}{8}$

b $\frac{1}{2} \times \frac{5}{8}$ **d** $\frac{3}{10} \times \frac{2}{15}$ **f** $\frac{4}{9} \times \frac{9}{10}$ **h** $\frac{9}{16} \times \frac{5}{9}$

3 Work out:

a $2 \div \frac{1}{7}$ **c** $12 \div \frac{1}{6}$ **e** $8 \div \frac{2}{3}$ **g** $18 \div \frac{3}{4}$

b $5 \div \frac{1}{4}$ **d** $45 \div \frac{5}{9}$ **f** $10 \div \frac{5}{8}$ **h** $32 \div \frac{4}{5}$

4 Work out:

a $\frac{5}{6} \div \frac{1}{3}$ **c** $\frac{7}{10} \div \frac{3}{5}$ **e** $\frac{2}{7} \div \frac{4}{7}$ **g** $\frac{9}{25} \div \frac{3}{5}$

b $\frac{5}{8} \div \frac{1}{4}$ **d** $\frac{2}{7} \div \frac{2}{7}$ **f** $\frac{2}{7} \div \frac{1}{7}$ **h** $\frac{4}{15} \div \frac{2}{3}$

5 Jared says that $\frac{3}{4} \div \frac{1}{2} = \frac{3}{8}$

Is he correct? Explain your answer.

6 Yasmin and Zoe are working out $\frac{9}{10} \times \frac{5}{6}$

Yasmin says the answer is $\frac{45}{60}$

Zoe says the answer is $\frac{3}{4}$

Who is correct? Explain your answer.

7 Lyn says, '6 divided by $\frac{1}{3}$ is 2.'

Is Lyn correct? Explain your answer.

8 Without working out the answers, arrange these calculations in order, the one with the smallest answer first and the one with the largest answer last.

$1 \times \frac{1}{3}$ $1 \div \frac{1}{3}$ $1 \times \frac{2}{3}$ $1 \div \frac{2}{3}$

9 Get Real!

David's recipe says that he needs two thirds of a cup of cream for some ice cream for four people. How much cream does he need if he wants to make ice cream for six people?

10 Get Real!

Diane has 4 yards of fabric to make some hats for a school sale. Each hat needs $\frac{3}{8}$ yard of fabric. How many hats can Diane make and how much fabric is left over?

8 Surds

1 Write these numbers in the form $\frac{a}{b}$, giving your answers in their lowest terms.

   a 0.8   **b** 11   **c** $3\frac{1}{4}$ **d** $0.\dot{7}$ **e** $0.\dot{1}6\dot{2}$

2 Which of these are rational, and which are irrational?

   a $\sqrt{2}$ **c** $\dfrac{\sqrt{10}}{11}$ **e** $\sqrt{10}+\sqrt{10}$

   b $\sqrt{49}$ **d** $\sqrt{10}\times\sqrt{10}$ **f** $\dfrac{\sqrt{12}}{\sqrt{3}}$

3 Simplify:

   a $\sqrt{27}$ **b** $\sqrt{63}$ **c** $\sqrt{32}$ **d** $\sqrt{147}$

4 Simplify:

   a $5\sqrt{2}+\sqrt{2}$ **c** $\sqrt{20}-\sqrt{5}$ **e** $\sqrt{50}-\sqrt{18}$ **g** $\sqrt{75}+\sqrt{27}$

   b $9\sqrt{5}-\sqrt{5}$ **d** $\sqrt{27}+\sqrt{3}$ **f** $6\sqrt{3}-\sqrt{48}$ **h** $\sqrt{12}+3\sqrt{3}-\sqrt{48}$

5 Jamilah says $4\times3\sqrt{2}=12\sqrt{8}=12\times2\sqrt{2}=24\sqrt{2}$. Josef says $4\times3\sqrt{2}=12\sqrt{2}$.

   Who is wrong, and where is the mistake?

6 Simplify:

   a $\sqrt{6}\times\sqrt{12}$ **c** $4\sqrt{3}\times3\sqrt{6}$ **e** $\dfrac{5\sqrt{10}}{\sqrt{5}}$ **g** $\sqrt{2}(4+\sqrt{8})$

   b $\sqrt{14}\times2\sqrt{7}$ **d** $\dfrac{\sqrt{20}}{\sqrt{5}}$ **f** $\sqrt{5}(2+\sqrt{5})$ **h** $(3+\sqrt{3})(2+\sqrt{3})$

7 Which of these are correct, and which are incorrect?

   a $\sqrt{6}+\sqrt{2}=\sqrt{8}=2\sqrt{2}$ **c** $\sqrt{6}\div\sqrt{2}=\sqrt{3}$

   b $\sqrt{6}\times\sqrt{2}=\sqrt{12}=2\sqrt{3}$ **d** $\sqrt{6}-\sqrt{2}=\sqrt{4}=2$

8 A cube has a total surface area of 48 cm². Find:

   a the surface area of one face

   b the length of an edge of the cube, giving your answer in its simplified surd form.

9 Find the odd one out in each row.

   a i $\sqrt{20}$ **ii** $2\sqrt{5}$ **iii** $\dfrac{\sqrt{40}}{2}$ **iv** $\sqrt{45} - \sqrt{5}$

   b i $\dfrac{\sqrt{30}}{\sqrt{3}}$ **ii** $\sqrt{12} - \sqrt{2}$ **iii** $\sqrt{2} \times \sqrt{5}$ **iv** $\dfrac{\sqrt{40}}{2}$

   c i $\sqrt{\dfrac{40}{5}}$ **ii** $\dfrac{2\sqrt{5} + 2\sqrt{5}}{\sqrt{5}}$ **iii** $\sqrt{2} + \sqrt{2}$ **iv** $\dfrac{2\sqrt{6}}{\sqrt{3}}$

10 Write $\sqrt{50} + \sqrt{18}$ in the form $a\sqrt{b}$.

Homework 2

1 Rationalise the denominators of these fractions:

   a $\dfrac{2}{\sqrt{3}}$ **c** $\dfrac{4}{2\sqrt{3}}$ **e** $\dfrac{3\sqrt{2}}{\sqrt{6}}$ **g** $\sqrt{\dfrac{5}{11}}$

   b $\dfrac{6}{\sqrt{3}}$ **d** $\dfrac{3\sqrt{5}}{5\sqrt{3}}$ **f** $\dfrac{3\sqrt{6}}{2\sqrt{3}}$ **h** $\dfrac{7\sqrt{7}}{2\sqrt{14}}$.

2 Show that $\dfrac{3}{\sqrt{3}} = \sqrt{3}$.

3 Find your way through this maze, only occupying spaces where the answer is correct.

Start	$\dfrac{2}{\sqrt{5}} = \dfrac{\sqrt{5}}{5}$	$\dfrac{3}{2\sqrt{3}} = \dfrac{\sqrt{3}}{3}$	$\sqrt{\dfrac{4}{9}} = \dfrac{2}{3}$	**End**
$\dfrac{1}{\sqrt{5}} = \dfrac{\sqrt{5}}{5}$	$\dfrac{4}{\sqrt{10}} = \dfrac{2\sqrt{5}}{10}$	$\dfrac{\sqrt{10}}{\sqrt{5}} = \sqrt{5}$	$\dfrac{12}{\sqrt{3}} = 4\sqrt{3}$	$\dfrac{1}{\sqrt{2}} = 2\sqrt{2}$
$\dfrac{4}{\sqrt{6}} = \dfrac{2\sqrt{6}}{3}$	$\dfrac{2}{\sqrt{3}} = \dfrac{2\sqrt{3}}{3}$	$\dfrac{3}{\sqrt{3}} = 3$	$\dfrac{a+\sqrt{a}}{\sqrt{a}} = \sqrt{a}+1$	$\dfrac{3}{\sqrt{2}} + \dfrac{1}{\sqrt{2}} = 2\sqrt{2}$
$\dfrac{\sqrt{2}}{\sqrt{3}} = \dfrac{\sqrt{3}}{3}$	$\dfrac{1}{4\sqrt{3}} = \dfrac{\sqrt{3}}{12}$	$\dfrac{2}{\sqrt{2a}} = \dfrac{\sqrt{2a}}{a}$	$\dfrac{5}{2\sqrt{3}} = \dfrac{5\sqrt{3}}{3}$	$\dfrac{2}{\sqrt{5}} + \dfrac{3}{\sqrt{5}} = \sqrt{5}$
$\dfrac{2a}{\sqrt{a}} = \sqrt{2a}$	$\dfrac{5}{\sqrt{2}} = \dfrac{\sqrt{10}}{2}$	$\dfrac{10}{\sqrt{5}} = 2\sqrt{5}$	$\dfrac{2}{\sqrt{10}} = 2$	$\dfrac{1}{\sqrt{2}} - \dfrac{1}{\sqrt{3}} = \dfrac{3\sqrt{2}-2\sqrt{3}}{6}$
$\dfrac{4}{\sqrt{2}} = \sqrt{2}$	$\dfrac{3}{\sqrt{7}} = \dfrac{7}{\sqrt{3}}$	$\dfrac{9}{\sqrt{3}} = 3\sqrt{3}$	$\dfrac{ab}{\sqrt{a}} = b\sqrt{a}$	$\dfrac{2\sqrt{3}}{\sqrt{2}} = \sqrt{6}$

4 What must you multiply $(\sqrt{5} - 2)$ by to get an answer of 1?

5 Show that $(1 + \sqrt{2})(1 - \sqrt{2}) = -1$

9 Representing data

Homework 1

1 Janesh undertakes a survey on packets of chocolate beans. He counts the number in each packet. His results are as follows:

30	31	30	30	29	32	41	29	30	31
30	28	30	31	30	30	30	30	31	30

  a Show this information in a stem-and-leaf diagram.

  b What is the most likely number of chocolate beans in a packet?

  c Which number in the list is likely to be an error?

2 The prices paid for sandwiches in a canteen are shown below:

£3.25 £2.65 £3.15 £1.95 £2.85 £2.65 £3.25 £3.75 £1.95 £2.95

Copy and complete the following stem-and-leaf diagram to show this information.

Prices paid for sandwiches

Stem (£)	Leaf (pence)
1	
2	
3	

Key: 3|25 represents £3.25

3 The marks obtained in a test were recorded as follows.

11 22 20 19 25 18 12 9 27 22 10 18 24 16 15 22

  a Show this information in an ordered stem-and-leaf diagram.

  b What was the least number of marks in the test?

  c Write down the mode of the marks in the test.

  d Write down the range of the marks in the test.

4   The marks scored in a test by 15 boys and 15 girls is shown in this back-to-back stem-and-leaf diagram.

Number of marks in a test

Leaf (units) Girls	Stem (tens)	Leaf (units) Boys
9	0	6 7 8 9
9 8 6 5 4 2 0	1	1 3 4 5 5 5 7 8 9
7 6 4 3 2 1	2	2 4
0	3	

Key: 3|2 represents
       23 marks

Key: 2|3 represents
       23 marks

a Calculate the median for the girls.

b Calculate the mode for the boys.

c Calculate the mean for the girls.

d Calculate the range for the boys.

e What can you say about the performance of girls and boys?

5   Andy measures the resting heartbeat of 15 children and 15 adults. His results are recorded in the table.

Resting heartbeat														
Child	83	71	83	76	79	88	81	73	83	69	94	87	80	89	85
Adult	75	80	79	69	70	73	84	75	65	75	78	69	67	81	74

a Show this information in a back-to-back stem-and-leaf diagram.

b Andy says that 'the older you are, the slower your resting heartbeat'. Use your data to check Andy's hypothesis.

6   The table shows the results of a survey to find student's favourite pets.

Pet	Tally
Cat	JHT JHT JHT JHT JHT
Dog	JHT JHT JHT JHT JHT II
Horse	JHT JHT IIII
Bird	JHT JHT JHT I
Fish	JHT III

Draw a pie chart to show the information.

7 Students at a college are asked to choose their favourite colour. Their choices are shown in the pie chart opposite:

A total of 45 students chose the colour blue.

a How many students were included in the survey?

b How many students chose red?

Twice as many students chose green as chose yellow.

c How many students chose green?

Favourite colour

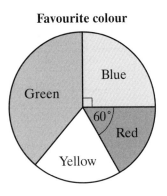

Homework 2

1 The table shows the time spent waiting at a clinic.

Draw a frequency diagram to represent the data.

Time, t (minutes)	Frequency
$0 \leqslant t < 10$	4
$10 \leqslant t < 20$	14
$20 \leqslant t < 30$	4
$30 \leqslant t < 40$	1

2 The frequency diagram shows the ages of people in a church.

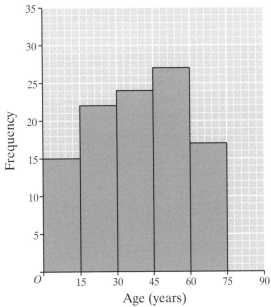

Ages of people in a church

Copy and complete this table to show this information.

Age, y (years)	Frequency
$0 \leqslant y < 15$	
$15 \leqslant y < 30$	
$30 \leqslant y < 45$	
$45 \leqslant y < 60$	
$60 \leqslant y < 75$	

3   The following table shows the temperature of a patient at different times of the day.

Time of day	10:00	11:00	12:00	13:00	14:00	15:00
Temperature (°F)	102.5	101.3	102	100.6	100.1	99.6

a Draw a line graph to show the temperature.

The normal temperature is 98.8 °F.

b At what time is the patient's temperature likely to return to normal?

4   The table shows the minimum and maximum temperatures at a seaside resort.

Day	Minimum temperature (°C)	Maximum temperature (°C)
Monday	15	19
Tuesday	17	22
Wednesday	14	21
Thursday	13	19
Friday	11	16

Draw a line graph to show:

a the minimum temperatures

b the maximum temperatures.

Use your graph to find:

c the day on which the lowest temperature was recorded

d the day on which the highest temperature was recorded.

5 **a** The table shows the quarterly phone bills for 2006 and 2007. The first two four-point moving averages are shown.

Copy the table and calculate the remaining four-point moving averages.

Year	2006	2006	2006	2006	2007	2007	2007	2007
Quarter	1st	2nd	3rd	4th	1st	2nd	3rd	4th
Cost	£115	£135	£103	£65	£101	£127	£43	£60
Four-point moving average		£104.50	£101.00					

b Show this information on a graph.

c What can you say about the trend?

6 Narinder's termly exam results are shown in the following table.

Year	2005	2006	2006	2006	2007	2007	2007
Session	Autumn	Spring	Summer	Autumn	Spring	Summer	Autumn
Results (%)	98	93	70	97	95	69	98

a Show this information on a graph.

b Use the information to calculate the three-point moving averages.

c Narinder says that her performance is improving. Is she correct? Give a reason for your answer.

7 The following table shows the mean number of sales of CDs and DVDs at a corner shop from 1998 to 2004.

Year	1998	1999	2000	2001	2002	2003	2004
CD sales	320	345	310	305	300	235	260
DVD sales	100	125	165	220	230	240	280

a Show this information on a graph.

b Construct a table showing the three-year moving average and plot the resulting trend lines.

c Comment on your results.

Homework 3

1 The table shows the heights of some trees.

Height (m)	Frequency
0 up to 2	6
2 up to 4	22
4 up to 8	15
8 up to 12	7

a Show this information on a cumulative frequency diagram.

b Use your cumulative frequency diagram to estimate:

i the median

ii the interquartile range.

2 The table shows the arm spans of students in a class.

Arm span (cm)	Frequency
$150 < l \leqslant 155$	3
$155 < l \leqslant 160$	9
$160 < l \leqslant 165$	13
$165 < l \leqslant 170$	17
$170 < l \leqslant 175$	8

a Show this information in a cumulative frequency diagram.

b Use your cumulative frequency diagram to estimate:

i the median

ii the interquartile range.

3 The table shows the wages of 40 staff in a small company.

Wages (£)	Frequency
$0 \leqslant x < 100$	5
$100 \leqslant x < 150$	11
$150 \leqslant x < 200$	15
$200 \leqslant x < 250$	7
$250 \leqslant x < 300$	0
$300 \leqslant x < 350$	2

a Show this information on a cumulative frequency diagram.

b Use your cumulative frequency diagram to estimate:

i the median

ii the interquartile range.

4 Andrea is completing her mathematics homework and draws this cumulative frequency diagram.

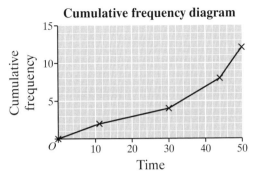

Cumulative frequency diagram

How can you tell that Andrea is wrong?
Give a reason for your answer.

5 Neil is comparing sentence lengths in newspapers and magazines, and has drawn this cumulative frequency diagram.

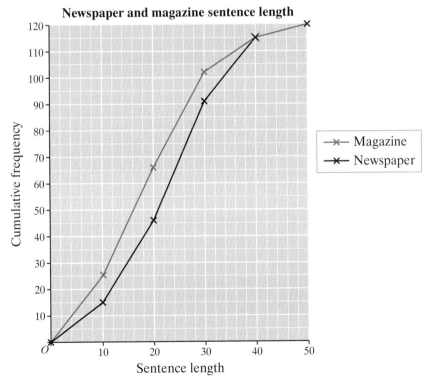

Newspaper and magazine sentence length

Which one has the longer sentences? Give a reason for your answer.

6 The waiting times at a dentist are recorded in the table below.

Time (min)	Frequency
$0 \leqslant t < 5$	8
$5 \leqslant t < 10$	12
$10 \leqslant t < 15$	7
$15 \leqslant t < 30$	3

a Show this information on a cumulative frequency diagram.

b Use your cumulative frequency diagram to estimate:

i the median

ii the interquartile range

iii the percentage of people waiting over 20 minutes.

7 The cumulative frequency diagram shows the time taken to complete a test.

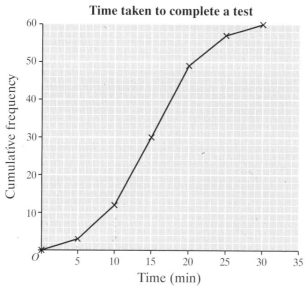

Complete the table to show the cumulative frequency and frequency.

Time (min)	Cumulative frequency	Frequency
$0 < t \leqslant 5$		
$5 < t \leqslant 10$		
$10 < t \leqslant 15$		
$15 < t \leqslant 20$		
$20 < t \leqslant 25$		
$25 < t \leqslant 30$		

8 For each of these cumulative frequency diagrams, draw the associated frequency diagram as a line graph.

Cumulative frequency	Frequency diagram
a	
b	
c	
d	

Homework 4

1 Copy the box plot and write the correct labels in the spaces.

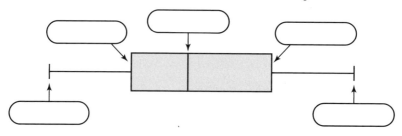

2 Draw a box plot of this data.

18	8	19	15	27	13	10	4	8	31	26	11	29	28	23

3 Draw a box plot of this data.

29	15	23	31	21	18	26	25	13	30	19

4 These box plots show the ages of shoppers in two clothes shops.

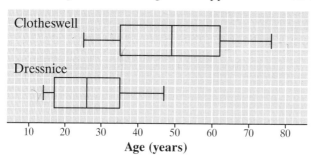

Copy and complete the table for the two shops.

	Clotheswell	Dressnice
Minimum age		
Maximum age		
Lower quartile		
Upper quartile		
IQR		
Median		
Range		

Compare the ages of the shoppers in the two shops.
What do you notice?

5 The cumulative frequency diagram shows the heights of 50 students.

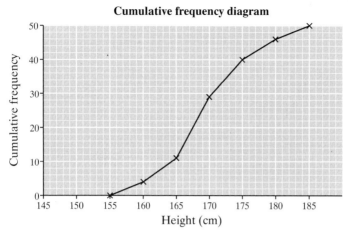

Cumulative frequency diagram

a Use the cumulative frequency diagram to estimate:

   i the median   **iii** the upper quartile.

   ii the lower quartile

b Draw a box plot for the data.

6 Draw the cumulative frequency diagram for the data shown in each box plot.
In each case use total frequency = 50

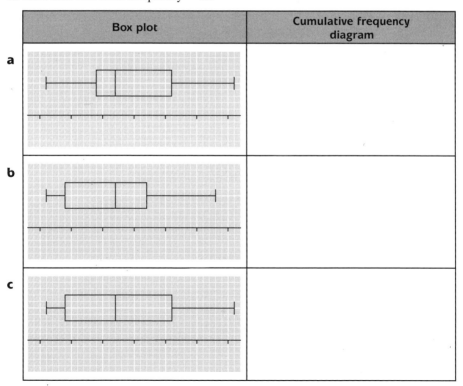

Box plot	Cumulative frequency diagram
a	
b	
c	

Homework 5

1   The histogram gives the heights of bushes in a garden.

Histogram

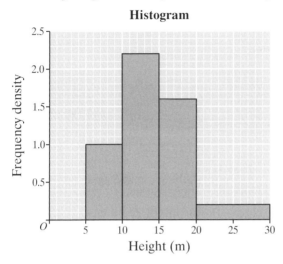

Height (m)

a How many bushes are there in the garden?

b How many bushes have heights between 5 cm and 15 cm?

2   The table shows the distances travelled by van drivers.

Distance (miles)	Frequency
$0 < d \leqslant 10$	8
$10 < d \leqslant 20$	14
$20 < d \leqslant 30$	22
$30 < d \leqslant 50$	18
$50 < d \leqslant 100$	8

Show this information as:

a a histogram

b a frequency polygon.

3 The weights of 50 students are recorded as follows.

Weight (kg)	Frequency
$40 \leqslant w < 42.5$	1
$42.5 \leqslant w < 45$	10
$45 \leqslant w < 50$	16
$50 \leqslant w < 55$	13
$55 \leqslant w < 65$	9
$65 \leqslant w < 75$	1

Show this information as:

a a histogram

b a frequency polygon.

4 Light bulbs are tested to see how long they last. Here are the results of 60 tests.

Time (hours)	Frequency
$600 \leqslant x < 700$	3
$700 \leqslant x < 800$	15
$800 \leqslant x < 850$	20
$850 \leqslant x < 900$	12
$900 \leqslant x < 1000$	8
$1000 \leqslant x < 1200$	2

Draw a frequency polygon to show this information.

5 The cumulative frequency diagram shows the waiting times for 30 patients at a dentist. Show this information in a histogram.

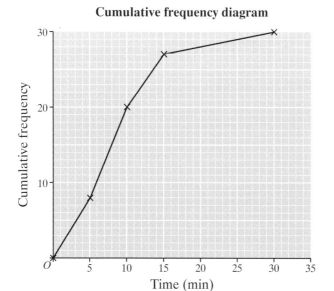

Cumulative frequency diagram

10 Scatter graphs

Homework 1

1 The graph shows the marks awarded by two judges in a competition.

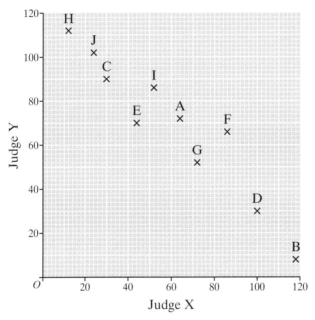

a Copy and complete the table for the marks awarded by the two judges.

	A	B	C	D	E	F	G	H	I	J
Judge X										
Judge Y										

b Are the two judges consistent? Give a reason for your answer.

2 For each of the following scatter graphs, match the diagram to the description.

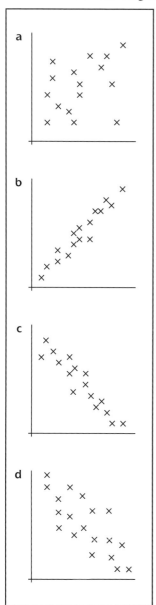

i Strong positive correlation

ii Strong negative correlation

iii No correlation

iv Weak positive correlation

v Weak negative correlation

3 For each of the following data sets:

    i describe the type and strength of correlation

    ii write a sentence explaining the relationship between the two sets.

  a The age of a person and their IQ.

  b The number of cars on the road and the time taken to get home.

  c Age and value of a computer.

  d The distance to the destination and the cost of a holiday.

4 The scatter graph shows a comparison of the prices of paintings in 2000 and 2006.

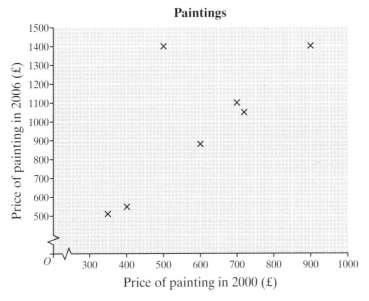

Paintings

a Describe the type and strength of correlation.

b Write a sentence explaining the relationship between the two sets of data.

c Does the relation hold for all of the paintings? Give a reason for your answer.

5 The table shows the ages and second-hand values of eight cars.

Age of car (years)	3	1	4	7	12	9	8	2
Value of car (£)	2900	4000	2100	1200	300	500	1400	3500

a Draw a scatter graph of the results.

b Describe the type and strength of correlation.

c Write a sentence explaining the relationship between the two sets of data.

6 The table shows the rainfall and the number of raincoats sold at a department store.

Amount of rainfall (mm)	0	1	2	5	6	9	11
Number of raincoats sold	12	25	48	56	63	85	98

a Draw a scatter graph of the results.

b Describe the type and strength of correlation.

c Write a sentence explaining the relationship between the two sets of data.

7 The table shows the history and physics results for nine students.

History (%)	10	20	76	74	40	62	70	26	19
Physics (%)	75	82	15	23	51	33	18	64	78

a Draw a scatter graph of the results.

b Describe the type and strength of correlation.

c Write a sentence explaining the relationship between the two sets of data.

Homework 2

1 The table shows the ages and second-hand values of eight cars.

Age of car (years)	3	1	4	7	11	9	8	2
Value of car (£)	2900	4000	2100	1200	300	500	1400	3500

a Draw a scatter graph and a line of best fit of the results.

b Use your line of best fit to estimate:

   i the value of a car if it is 10 years old

   ii the age of a car if its value is £2000.

2 The table shows the rainfall and the number of raincoats sold at a department store.

Amount of rainfall (mm)	0	1	2	5	6	9	11
Number of raincoats sold	12	25	48	56	63	85	98

a Draw a scatter graph and a line of best fit of the results.

b Use your line of best fit to estimate:

   i the number of raincoats sold for 8 mm of rainfall

   ii the amount of rainfall if 50 raincoats are sold.

3 The table shows the history and physics results for nine students.

History (%)	10	20	76	74	40	62	70	26	19
Physics (%)	75	82	15	23	51	33	18	64	78

a Draw a scatter graph and a line of best fit of the results.

b Use your line of best fit to estimate:

   i the physics result for a student who scores 54 in history

   ii the history result for a student who scores 90 in physics.

c Which of these two answers is likely to be a better estimate? Give a reason for your answer.

4 The scatter graph shows a line of best fit for the science and maths results of eight students.

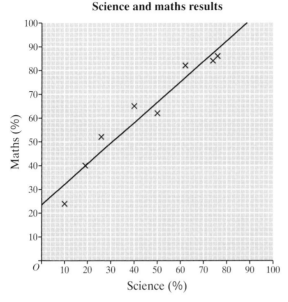

Science and maths results

a Use the line of best fit to estimate:

  i the maths result for a student who scores 60 in science

  ii the science result for a student who scores 100 in maths.

b Which of these two answers is likely to be a better estimate? Give a reason for your answer.

5 The table shows the engine sizes and maximum speeds of eight cars.

Engine size (cc)	Maximum speed (mph)
1100	80
1800	125
2900	142
1400	107
1300	96
1000	85
2500	135
2000	131

a Draw a scatter graph and the line of best fit of the results.

b Describe the relationship between a car's engine size and its maximum speed.

c Use your line of best fit to estimate:

  i the maximum speed of a car with an engine size of 1500 cc

  ii the engine size of a car whose maximum speed is 150 mph.

d Explain why your last answer might not be accurate.

6 A line of best fit shows the relationship between two sets of data in an experiment.

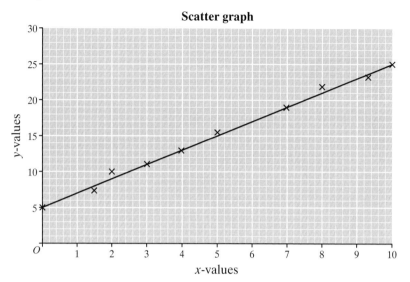

Scatter graph

a Use the line of best fit to estimate:

i the value of *y* when *x* = 7

ii the value of *x* when *y* = 22.

b By considering the equation of the line of best fit, explain how you would find the value of *y* when *x* = 20.

7 The following table gives the age and speed of 15 people over a distance of 100 m.

Age (years)	12	5	8	10	11	12	15	14	18	28	34	38	42	39	33
Speed (m/s)	5.4	1.8	3.6	4.2	5.8	6.1	6.8	7.4	8.1	7.3	6.8	7.4	6.4	7.1	5.9

a Draw a scatter graph of the results.

b Draw a line of best fit for the results.

c Describe the relationship between speed and age.

d Find an estimate for the speed of someone aged 13 years.

Homework 1

1 Follow the flowchart for each of these shapes.

SQUARE   RHOMBUS   KITE   TRAPEZIUM
PARALLELOGRAM   RECTANGLE

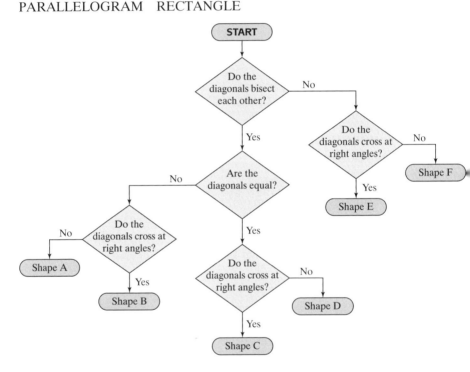

Write your answers as: Shape A is a ...

2 Calculate the angles marked with letters in the diagrams below. You will need to use the properties of diagonals. Explain how you know the size of the angles.

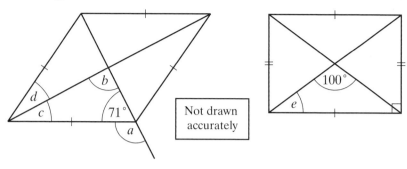

Not drawn accurately

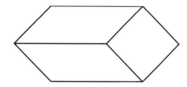

3 The diagram shows two congruent parallelograms and a square.

Calculate the sizes of the angles in the parallelogram.

4 A trapezium has an angle of 78° and another of 123°.
What are the other two angles?

5 A teacher asks the class to draw a parallelogram with angles of 40° and 140°.

  a Alice draws one with all sides the same length. What shape has she drawn?

  b Bella mistakenly puts her two angles of 40° next to each other. What shape does she draw?

  c Chris makes a mistake and draws one angle of 30° instead of 40°. He gets the 140° angles correct. What size is his fourth angle, and what shape has he drawn?

Homework 2

1 Calculate the angles marked with letters in the diagram.
Give reasons for your answers.

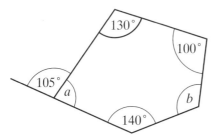

Not drawn
accurately

2 A hexagon has three angles of 130° and two of 112°.
Calculate the sixth angle.

3 A regular polygon has an exterior angle of 20°.
How many sides does it have?

4 Draw a circle with a radius of 6 cm. Draw a regular decagon that just fits
inside the circle.

5 The diagram below shows a regular octagon ABCDEFGH and a regular
hexagon DCIJKL.

Calculate the angles:

a HAB   **c** BCI   **e** LKC

b CIJ   **d** BCG   **f** GCK

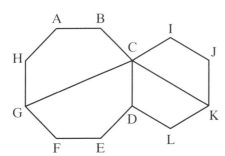

6 Explain why a regular hexagon will tessellate, but a regular pentagon will not.

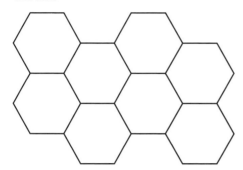

7 **a** A regular polygon has interior angles of 150°. How many sides does the polygon have?

    b The polygon will tessellate with another regular polygon. What is the other regular polygon?

8 This regular octagon has been divided into a kite and two trapeziums.

Calculate the four angles of the kite.

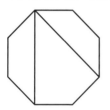

12 Indices and standard form

1 David says that the square of a number is always bigger than the number.
Is he correct?
Give a reason for your answer.

2 Write these in index notation.

    a $6 \times 6 \times 6 \times 6 \times 6$ **d** 10

    b $2 \times 2 \times 2 \times 2 \times 2 \times 2 \times 2 \times 2 \times 2 \times 2$ **e** $\frac{1}{4}$

    c $17 \times 17 \times 17$ **f** $\left(\frac{1}{4}\right)^2$

3 Find the value of each of the following.

    a 9^2 **d** 10^1 **g** 1^3 **j** 100^{-1}

    b 2^8 **e** 4^0 **h** 4^{-1} **k** $\left(\frac{1}{3}\right)^2$

    c 3^3 **f** 1000^0 **i** 5^{-3} **l** $\left(\frac{2}{3}\right)^2$

4 Find the value of each of the following.

    a 2^{20} **d** 8^3 **g** $2^{10} - 2^9$

    b 2^{21} **e** 5^{10} **h** $4^8 \times 2^{-16}$

    c 3^8 **f** -2^6 **i** $10^{51} \div 10^{49}$

5 Simplify the following.

    a $3^8 \times 3^{11}$ **c** $\dfrac{3^7}{3^6}$ **e** $\left(\left(1^2\right)^3\right)^4$

    b $12^4 \times 12^{-2}$ **d** $1.5^{10} \div 1.5^9$ **f** $(3.1^2)^{10}$

6 Calculate:

    a $64^{\frac{1}{2}}$ **d** $27^{\frac{2}{3}}$ **g** $64^{\frac{1}{6}}$ **j** $1^{\frac{1}{5}}$

    b $169^{\frac{1}{2}}$ **e** $-27^{\frac{2}{3}}$ **h** $9^{-\frac{1}{2}}$ **k** $1^{-\frac{1}{5}}$

    c $125^{\frac{1}{3}}$ **f** $(-27)^{\frac{2}{3}}$ **i** $(-216)^{\frac{2}{3}}$

7 Use your calculator to work out the following.

    a 70^2 **b** $81^{-0.5}$ **c** $625^{1.5}$ **d** $10\,000^{-0.25}$

8 Simplify the following.

    a $a^5 \times a^3$ **c** $\dfrac{c^{11}}{c}$ **e** $q^{10} \div q^{11}$

    b $b^{10} \times b^6$ **d** $p^{100} \div p^{99}$ **f** $(s^2)^4$

9 Simplify the following.

    a $6x^3 \times 5x^6$ **b** $\dfrac{4a^9}{8a^5}$ **c** $5b^3 \times 2b^7$ <u>**d**</u> $(3b^4)^5$

<u>**10**</u> The number 256 can be written as 16^2 in index form.

    Write down five other ways that 256 can be written in index form.

11 Tariq is investigating square numbers. He says that square numbers cannot end in a 2. Is he correct? Give a reason for your answer.

Homework 2

Apart from questions 6 and 8, this is a non-calculator exercise.

1 Write the following standard form numbers in ordinary form.

    a 8×10^2 **c** 4.0115×10^2 **e** 2.25×10^{-6}

    b 5.1×10^3 **d** 5×10^{-3}

2 Write the following ordinary form numbers in standard form.

    a 362 000   **c** 1 000 100   **e** 0.1

    b 45 500 000 000   **d** 0.000055

3 Get Real!

    The distance of Saturn from the Sun is 1 429 400 000 km.

    Write this distance in standard form.

4 Get Real!

The diameter of one molecule is 8.33×10^{-9} metres.

Write this number in ordinary form.

5 Get Real!

The following table shows the masses of the planets in the solar system.

Planet	Mass (kg)
Mercury	3.3×10^{23}
Venus	4.9×10^{24}
Earth	6.0×10^{24}
Mars	6.4×10^{23}
Jupiter	1.9×10^{27}
Saturn	5.7×10^{26}
Uranus	8.7×10^{25}
Neptune	1.0×10^{26}
Pluto	1.3×10^{22}

Place the planets in order of mass with the lightest first.

6 Write the number 80^4 in standard form.

7 Calculate the following, giving your answers in standard form.

a $(4 \times 10^5) \times (2 \times 10^{11})$

d $\dfrac{4 \times 10^6}{2 \times 10^1}$

b $(5 \times 10^3) \times (1.5 \times 10^9)$

e $\dfrac{1.1 \times 10^6}{4.4 \times 10^{-3}}$

c $(2.4 \times 10^5) \times (2 \times 10^{-6})$

f $\dfrac{5.2 \times 10^5}{1.3 \times 10^8}$

8 Use your calculator to find the following, giving your answers in standard form.

a $(4.1 \times 10^4) \times (2.2 \times 10^3)$

d $(1.6 \times 10^4)^3$

b $(5.8 \times 10^5) \times (2.3 \times 10^2)$

e $\dfrac{4.4 \times 10^6}{2 \times 10^8}$

c $(2.12 \times 10^{-2}) \times (7.7 \times 10^{-6})$

9 Given that $p = 4.5 \times 10^3$ and $q = 2 \times 10^{-1}$, calculate:

a $p \times q$ **c** $p + q$ **e** p^2

b $p \div q$ **d** $p - q$

13 Sequences

1 Write the term-to-term rule for each of the following sequences.

    a 7, 11, 15, 19 ...   **d** 0.1, 1, 10, 100, ...   **g** 21, 17, 13, 9, ...

    b 0, 9, 18, 27, ...   **e** 2.1, 3.2, 4.3, 5.4, ...   **h** 8, 4, 2, 1, $\frac{1}{2}$ ...

    c 2, 4, 8, 16, 32, ...   **f** 3, 5.5, 8, 10.5, ...

2 Write the term-to-term rule for the following diagrams.

    What is the special name given to the sequence of numbers from these diagrams?

3 Write the first five terms of the sequence whose nth term is:

    a $n + 7$ **d** $n^2 - 5$ **g** $n^2 + 2$

    b $3n$ **e** $2n^2$ **h** $\dfrac{n + 1}{n + 2}$

    c $5n - 4$ **f** $3n - 7$

4 Copy and complete the following table.

Pattern (n)	Diagram	Number of matchsticks (m)
1		4 matchsticks
2		7 matchsticks
3		10 matchsticks
4		
5		

    a What do you notice about the pattern of matches above?

    b Write the formula for the number of matches (m) in the nth pattern.

5 Write the *n*th term in each of the following linear sequences.

  a 1, 2, 3, 4, ...   **d** 33, 31, 29, 27, ...   **g** 1.5, 4, 6.5, 9, ...

  b 0, 4, 8, 12, ...   **e** 1000, 995, 990, ...   **h** −13, −5, 3, 11, ...

  c 7, 13, 19, 25, ...   **f** −4, −1, 2, 5, ...

6 Write the formula for the number of squares in the *n*th pattern.

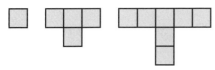

7 Write the *n*th term in each of the following non-linear sequences.

  a 1, 4, 9, 16, ...   **c** 11, 14, 19, 26, ...   **e** 2, 9, 28, 65, 126, ...

  b 0, 3, 8, 15, ...   **d** 1, 8, 27, 64, 125, ...   **f** 10, 100, 1000, ...

8 Write the *n*th term in each of the following sequences.

  a $1 \times 2 \times 3, 2 \times 3 \times 4, 3 \times 4 \times 5, ...$ **c** $\frac{2}{4}, \frac{3}{5}, \frac{4}{6}, \frac{5}{7}, ...$

  b $\frac{1}{2}, \frac{1}{3}, \frac{1}{4}, \frac{1}{5}, ...$ **d** 0.01, 0.02, 0.03, 0.04, ...

14 Coordinates

1 Write down the coordinates of the points where these lines cross.

a $x = 3$ and $y = 1$ **d** $x = 0$ and $y = -3$

b $x = -5$ and $y = 2$ **e** $x = -4.5$ and $y = -2.5$

c $x = -3$ and $y = -7$ **f** $y = -3$ and $y = x$

2 Look at this rule: The y-coordinate must be three more than the x-coordinate.

These two points fit the rule: $(1, 4)$ and $(-2, 1)$.

Write down three more pairs of coordinates that fit the rule.

Plot the points on a coordinate grid.

What is the equation of the line that passes through all the points?

3 Kazu says that the point $(3, 6)$ is on the line $y = x + 3$.

Bob says that the point $(3, 6)$ is on the line $y - x = 3$.

Who is right?

4 Where do these pairs of lines intersect?

a $x = 4$ and $y = x + 2$ **d** $y = 4$ and $y = x + 2$

b $x = -2$ and $y = 2x$ **e** $y = -3$ and $y = 2x - 3$

c $x = 5$ and $y = 2x - 3$ **f** $y = 2x$ and $y = x + 2$

5 For each of these grids, write the equation of the line.

a

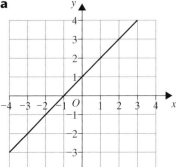

d

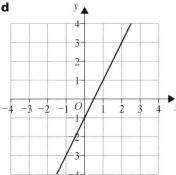

b

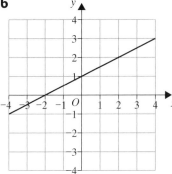

e

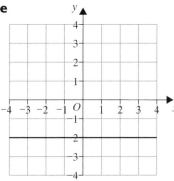

c

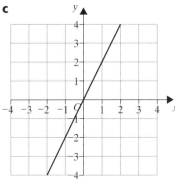

f

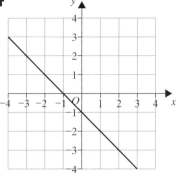

6 Find the equation of the line that passes through

   a $(0, 2)$ and $(2, 6)$ **c** $(1, 3)$ and $(4, 9)$ **e** $(2, 5)$ and $(4, -1)$

   b $(0, 3)$ and $(2, -3)$ **d** $(1, 4)$ and $(3, 2)$ **f** $(1, 4)$ and $(3, 7)$.

Homework 2

1 Work out the coordinates of the point halfway between (2, 10) and (4, 2).

2 Work out the coordinates of the point halfway between (2, −7) and (5, 3).

3 If A is the point (2, −4) and B is the point (−3, −3), what are the coordinates of the midpoint of the line AB?

4 Jon says that the point (−2.5, 3) is halfway between (−4, 9) and (−1, −15). Is he correct?

5 X is the midpoint of the line AB. The coordinates of X are (−3, 3). B is the point (1, −2). What are the coordinates of A?

6 Find your way through the maze by only occupying rectangles where M is the midpoint of AB. (No diagonal moves allowed.)

1 START	2 A(5, 2) B(3, 4) M(4, 3)	3 A(−2, 1) B(3, −4) M(0.5, −1.5)	4 A(4, 7) B(−2, −3) M(1, 2)	5 A(−1, 9) B(−5, 2) M(−3, 4.5)	6 A(3, 2) B(2, −3) M(2.5, 0.5)
7 A(4, 1) B(2, −2) M(3, 0.5)	8 A(−1, 2) B(2, −3) M(0.5, 0.5)	9 A(1, 3) B(2, −2.5) M(1.5, 0.5)	10 A(−1.7, 3.2) B(1.1, −2.6) M(−0.3, 0.3)	11 A(2, −0.8) B(−1, 0.9) M(0.5, 0.05)	12 A(6, 1) B(−6, −2) M(0, −0.5)
13 A(5, −4) B(−3, 4) M(1, 0)	14 A(−3, −2) B(2, −6) M(−0.5, −4)	15 A(−1.3 2.4) B(−1.2, 9) M(−1.25, 5.7)	16 A(2, 7) B(−3, 4) M(−0.5, 6.5)	17 A(3, −2) B(3, 2) M(6, 0)	18 A(−2, 1) B(−12, 5) M(−7, 3)
19 A(7, 0) B(0, 3) M(3.5, 1.5)	20 A(−1, −2.4) B(−2, 4.2) M(−1.5, 1.1)	21 A(7, −1) B(−4, −8) M(1.5, −4.5)	22 A(−8, 4) B(4, 2) M(−2, 3)	23 A(3, −3) B(1, −2) M(2, −2.5)	24 A(1.2, 2.7) B(2.4, 1.3) M(1.8, 2)
25 A(−2, −2) B(1, 5.8) M(−0.5, 1.9)	26 A(−3, −2.4) B(2, 6) M(−0.5, 1.8)	27 A(1, 2.3) B(−2, −6.2) M(0.5, −1.95)	28 A(0, 4.2) B(−2, 3.2) M(1, 3.7)	29 A(−1, 2.5) B(3, −0.1) M(2, 1.2)	30 A(2.6, 1.7) B(−1.4, 1.1) M(−0.6, 1.4)
31 A(91, 36) B(19, 8) M(50, 22)	32 A(5, −2) B(−3, 3) M(1, 0.5)	33 A(1, 3) B(−6, −3) M(−2.5, 0)	34 A(−2.4, 1.4) B(−2.2, −0.3) M(−2.3, 0.55)	35 A(0.2, −3) B(−2.3, 1) M(−1.05, −1)	36 END

7 **a** C is the midpoint of AB, where A is the point (4, 1) and B is (−2, 7). Find the coordinates of C.

b What is the equation of the line AB?

c C is also the midpoint of the line EF, where E is the point (2, 3). Find the coordinates of F.

Homework 3

1 **a** In the diagram, A is the point (0, 4, 2). D is the point (5, 0, 0).

Write down the coordinates of points B and C.

   b What are the coordinates of the midpoints of

   i OD

   ii CD

   iii AB

   iv OB?

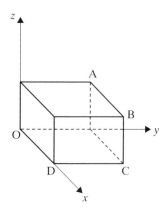

2 The diagram shows a triangular prism.

The triangular ends are isosceles.

The height of the prism is 8 units.

The base of the triangle AB is 5 units.

The length of the prism OA is 6 units.

Write down the coordinates of A, B, C and D.

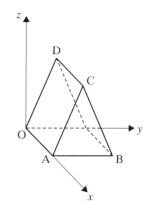

3 A large cuboid has these measurements:

OG = 12 cm, OE = 10 cm, OA = 8 cm.

A square hole of side 3 cm goes right through the cuboid.

J is the point (12, 4, 2.5).

Write down the coordinates of A, B, C, D, E, F, G and H.

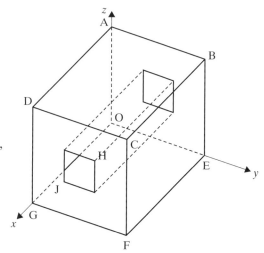

4 A cuboid has three of its vertices at (4, 1, 0), (4, 1, 6) and (2, 5, 0).

Find the coordinates of the other five vertices. As always, drawing a diagram will make it much easier.

5 The diagram shows three cubes.

The bottom cube has sides of length 8 cm, and has a vertex at (0, 0, 0).

The centre cube has sides of length 6 cm, and sits exactly in the middle of the bottom cube.

The top cube sits exactly in the middle of the centre cube, and has sides of length 4 cm.

What are the coordinates of the four top vertices of the top cube?

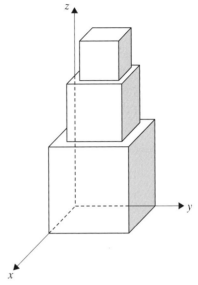

6 The diagram shows a cube.

The coordinates of A are (4, 0, 5), and B is at (0, 3, 5).

Find the coordinates of C, D, G and H.

(A diagram of the plan view will help.)

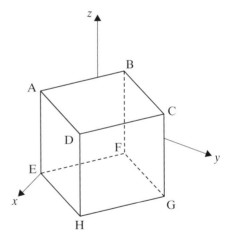

7 A rectangular board rests against a wall as shown. The coordinates of the corners are A(0, 3, 6), B(4, 0, 6), C(8, 2, 0) and D(4, 5, 0).

a Find the midpoints of each edge, AB, BC, CD and DA.

b Find the coordinates of M, the midpoint of AC.

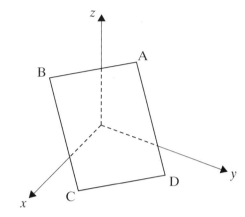

15 Collecting data

1   For each of the following state whether the data is quantitative or qualitative.

   a Ages of people.

   b Favourite film ever!

   c Goals scored in a school hockey match.

   d Students' favourite teacher at a school.

   e The number of police at a football match.

   f The time it takes to get home.

   g The softness of a pile of towels.

2   For each of the following say whether the data is discrete or continuous.

   a Ages of people.

   b Goals scored in a school hockey match.

   c The number of votes in a council election.

   d The amount of water consumed by a household.

   e The viewing figures for a TV programme.

   f The time it takes to get home.

   g The number of stars that can be seen in the sky.

3   Connect each of the following to its proper description. The first one has been done for you.

| Ages of lions at London Zoo |
| People's favourite cake at a show |
| Points scored in 10 darts matches |
| The weights of 12 newly born puppies |
| The favourite building of people in Britain |
| The average speed of train journeys into London |
| The number of hours spent driving a day |
| A person's shirt collar size |
| The cost of bread |
| Rainfall at a seaside resort |

| Quantitative and discrete |
| Qualitative |
| Quantitative and continuous |

4 The following questions are taken from different surveys.

Write down one criticism of each question.

Rewrite the question in a more suitable form.

a How many hours of homework do you complete each week?

Less than 1 hour ☐   More than 1 hour ☐

b What is your favourite colour?

Red ☐   Blue ☐

c How old are you?

Under 16 ☐   Under 21 ☐   Under 40 ☐

d You do like mathematics don't you?

Yes ☐   No ☐

e What is your favourite magazine?

Hello ☐   What car? ☐

5 Write down one advantage and one disadvantage of carrying out a personal (face-to-face) survey.

6 Write down a definition and give an example of each of the following kinds of data.

a Quantitative

b Qualitative

c Continuous

d Discrete

7 Give one advantage and one disadvantage of:

a primary data

b secondary data.

Homework 2

1 Which sampling methods are most appropriate for the following surveys?

Give a reason for each answer.

a The average weight of sheep on a farm with 1000 sheep.

b The favourite building of people in your town.

c The average amount of time spent on homework each week by students in your school.

d The average hand span of students in a school.

e The views of villagers on a new shopping centre.

f Information on voting intentions at a general election.

2 The following questions are taken from different surveys.

Write down one criticism of each question and explain how you would improve it.

a A company wants to find out if people like a new bar of chocolate they have made.

They stop people in the street and ask them to try it.

They give everyone a questionnaire asking them to write everything they like about the new bar.

b A London football club wants to build a new football stadium.

They carry out a survey in central London.

They ask 1000 people if they think it will be a good idea.

c Local commuters are trying to get an improved train service into London.

They collect signatures on the train one morning.

Three quarters of the respondents say that the train service could be improved.

d Jenny is collecting information on waiting times at her local health centre.

She gets permission from the doctors to undertake her survey.

She arrives one morning and makes a note of how long each patient waits.

e You want to find out if people like motor racing.

You carry out a face-to-face survey.

You ask 100 people watching the British Grand Prix at Silverstone.

f Tina is conducting a survey for the school magazine.

She wants to know about students' favourite colours for a new school uniform.

She asks 80 students from Year 7 and 70 students from Year 10 using random sampling.

3 A club wishes to undertake a survey of its members on whether to start serving food on the premises.

a Explain how you would take:

i a convenience sample of 100 members

ii a random sample of 100 members

iii a stratified sample of 100 members.

b Which is the most appropriate sampling method?
Give a reason for your answer.

4 A police force employs 200 female and 2300 male police officers. They wish to take a sample of 140 police officers to see what they do in their spare time.

Explain how you would take:

a a random sample of 140 police officers

b a systematic sample of 140 police officers

c a stratified sample of 140 police officers.

d Which is the most appropriate sampling method? Give a reason for your answer.

5 Sally wishes to carry out a stratified sample of 80 people from students at her school.

Year	7	8	9	10	11
Number	120	150	150	180	200

How many students should she sample from each year group?

6 The table shows the number of people employed in a store.

Occupation	Management	Office	Security	Sales
Number	5	10	25	160

a Explain why a random sample of the employees might not be suitable.

b Explain how you would take a stratified sample of size 40.

c Explain how you would take a stratified sample of size 30.

16 Percentages

Calculate:

1 30% of 50 cm

2 15% of £70

3 75% of 9.6 m

4 $17\frac{1}{2}$% of £540

5 Work out the interest on £1000 for 2 years at $4\frac{1}{2}$% per annum.

6 Work out the amount if £500 is invested for 4 years at 3% per annum.

7 Get Real!
Todd is paid £350 per week.

He gets a 4% pay rise.

What is his new weekly pay?

8 Get Real!
A package holiday is priced at £760.

Julie gets a 10% discount for booking before the end of January.

How much does she pay?

9 Get Real!
Chris has 50 books on his shelves.

Jenny has 12% more books.

How many books has Jenny got?

10 Get Real!
A train ticket is priced at £48.

In the new year the cost increases by $2\frac{1}{2}$%.

What is the new cost of the train ticket?

Calculate:

11 84% of 35 kg

12 27% of 60 cm

13 130% of £35.50

14 $37\frac{1}{2}$% of £11.50

15 Work out the interest on £6520 for 4 years at 3.8% per annum.

16 Find the total owed if £3575 is borrowed for 3 years at 14.3% per annum.

17 Get Real!
Sarah's salary is £13 575 per year.
Her annual bonus is $1\frac{3}{4}$% of her salary.
How much does she earn altogether?

18 Get Real!
Jack sells computers.
He is paid commission of $8\frac{1}{4}$% on his sales.
Last year he sold computers worth £85 496.
How much was his commission?

Homework 2

1 A football team has a supporters club with 400 members.
45% of the members are female.
20% of the female members are over 50.
How many females over 50 belong to the club?

2 Sam earns £1100 per month.
On average, he spends 30% of this at AqaMart.
15% of his AqaMart spending is on frozen foods.
How much does Sam spend on frozen food?

3 There are 75 ducks on a lake.

40% of them are drakes.

70% of the drakes are mallards.

How many mallard drakes are on the lake?

 4 Lisa bought a car for £20 000.

It depreciated by 30% in the first year and 35% in the second year.

What was it worth after two years?

 5 Jake started a new job in March, on £250 per week.

After three months, he was given a pay rise of 24%.

In October, all employees were given a 5% pay rise.

What did Jake get paid in October?

 6 Mathsville has 54 000 people eligible to vote.

65% of them voted in the last election.

37% of the votes cast were for Einstein.

How many votes did Einstein get?

 7 Dan bought an antique table for £3785.

A year later, its value had gone up by 22%.

In the following year, its value went up by 33%.

What was the table worth at the end of the second year?

 8 In 2003, HouseMasters sold 325 houses.

In 2004, their sales fell by 34%.

In 2005, sales went down again by $37\frac{1}{2}$%.

How many houses did they sell in 2005?

 9 Aisha bought shares worth £4500.

A year later their value had fallen by 3.73%.

In the following year, their value went up by 3.14%.

What were the shares worth after two years?

 10 If Aisha's shares went up by 3.73% in the second year, would they be worth £4500 again?

Explain your answer.

Homework 3

1 Find the compound interest on £300 invested for 2 years at 5% per annum.

2 Find the compound interest on £5000 invested for 2 years at 4% per annum.

3 £5000 is invested at 6% per annum compound interest.

Find the amount at the end of 2 years.

4 **a** £2000 is invested at 8% per annum compound interest.

Find the amount at the end of 3 years.

b Compare this investment with the same principal earning simple interest at $5\frac{1}{2}$% per annum over the same period of time.

5 Find the compound interest on £750 invested for 4 years at 3% per annum.

6 Find the compound interest on £3500 invested for 3 years at 8.2% per annum.

7 £9000 is invested at $6\frac{1}{4}$% per annum compound interest.

Find the amount at the end of 5 years.

8 £4000 is invested at 7% per annum compound interest.

After how many years will this amount to more than £6000?

9 The population of Geometeria is 654 000 and is growing by 9% per annum each year.

How many years will it take for the population to reach a million?

Homework 4

1 Express 32p as a percentage of 40p.

2 Express 17 g as a percentage of 20 g.

3 Express 35p as a percentage of £5.

4 Express 4 mm as a percentage of 10 cm.

5 Express 22 cm as a percentage of half a metre.

6 **Get Real!**
The price of a packet of cereal goes up from £1.40 to £1.54
Find the percentage increase.

7 **Get Real!**
The rent on Jade's flat goes up from £80 per week to £84 per week.
Find the percentage increase.

8 **Get Real!**
In the autumn term, Sean scored 15 goals.
In the spring term he scored 21 goals.
Find the percentage increase.

9 **Get Real!**
In a spring sale, the price of a coat is reduced from £60 to £42.
Find the percentage reduction.

10 **Get Real!**
Tim bought 100 fluffy toys at 50p each.
He sold 65 of them at £1.20 each.
a How much did he pay for the toys?
b How much money did he get from selling the toys?
c Find the profit as a percentage of his costs.

11 Express 5 cm as a percentage of 14 cm.

12 Express £19.25 as a percentage of £44.

13 Express 39p as a percentage of £19.50.

14 Express 216 g as a percentage of 4.8 kg.

15 Express 85 cm^2 as a percentage of 3 m^2.

16 Get Real!

The price of a hardback book is £15.

The paperback edition of the same book is £7.95

Express the difference as a percentage of the hardback price.

17 Get Real!

In March, Anna's sales totalled £44 000.

In April her sales were £36 960.

Find the percentage decrease.

18 Get Real!

Errol buys a car for £2450 and does some repairs.

He sells the car for £2950.

Find his percentage profit.

19 Get Real!

Kate bought 150 antique plates for £28 each.

She sold 98 of them for £54 each and a further 24 for £35 each.

a How much did it cost to buy the plates?

b How much money did she get from selling the plates?

c Find the profit as a percentage of her costs.

20 Get Real!

Tom bought a box of 60 old records for £40.

He sold 22 of them for £1.99 each.

Of these 14 were cracked and he sold the rest at three for a pound.

Calculate Tom's percentage profit.

Homework 5

1 Toys have been reduced by 20% in a sale.

Find the original price of these items.

a A doll priced at £4.80

b A train set priced at £12

c Wooden bricks priced at £6.80

2 Kylie has had a 10% pay rise.

She is now paid £264 per week.

How much was she paid before the rise?

3 Sarfraz is a car salesman.

In 2005 his sales amounted to £270 000.

This was an 8% increase on 2004.

What was his sales total in 2004?

4 The cost of Tara's train fare to work has gone up by $7\frac{1}{2}$%.

It is now £2.58

What was her train fare before the rise?

5 The population of Toptown has gone up by 43% over the last 5 years.

It is now 50 765.

What was the population 5 years ago?

6 A plumber offers a 3% discount if customers pay him within 7 days.

Mrs Matheson paid £54.32 on the day after the job was done.

What was the bill before discount?

7 After other deductions, Gary pays tax on his wages at 22%.

His take-home pay is £214.50 per week.

What was his wage before tax was deducted?

8 Lucy has been promoted at work and has had two pay rises this year.

The first was 8% and the second was 5%.

Her annual salary is now £16 840.

What was her salary before the first pay rise?

17 Equations

Solve these equations.

1 $4x - 1 = 2x + 8$

2 $5y - 4 = y + 6$

3 $3z - 7 = 10 - 2z$

4 $2 - t = 2t + 8$

5 $p + 2 = 5 - 3p$

6 $1 + 2q = 11 - 3q$

7 $3 + 7a = 5 - 3a$

8 $5b - 10 = 8b - 1$

9 $3c - 5 = 2 - 4c$

10 $2 + d = 5d + 4$

11 $12 - 3e = 6 - 5e$

12 $9f + 7 = 1 + 5f$

13 Jade solves the equation $5x - 3 = 9 - x$ and gets the answer $x = 3$.
Can you find Jade's mistake?

14 Tim solves the equation $4y + 7 = 9 - 2y$ and gets the answer $y = 3$.
Can you find Tim's mistake? Give a reason for your answer.

15 $4z - 11 = \blacksquare - z$
The answer to this equation is $z = 4$.
What is the number under the ink blob?

16 $2a + \blacksquare = 3 - a$
The answer to this equation is $a = -2$.
What is the number under the ink blob?

17 If $b = 3$, find the value of $4b - 7$.
Hence explain why $b = 3$ is not the solution of the equation
$4b - 7 = 4 - 3b$.

18 If $c = -2$, find the value of $9 - 3c$.
Hence explain why $c = -2$ is not the solution of the equation
$2c + 11 = 9 - 3c$.

19 Jon thinks of a number, trebles it and subtracts 4.

The answer is 26.

Write this as an equation.

Solve the equation to find Jon's number.

20 Zoë thinks of a number, multiplies it by 7 and adds 45. The answer is 3.

Write this as an equation.

Solve the equation to find Zoë's number.

21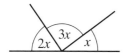

22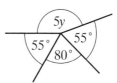

Write down an equation in x.

Solve your equation.

Write down an equation in y.

Solve your equation.

23 The mean of the numbers 5, 12, 30, 8, 23 and p is 16.

Write an equation and solve it to find the value of p.

24 q is an even number.

  a Write expressions for the next two even numbers in terms of q.

The sum of these three consecutive even numbers is 42.

  b Write an equation and solve it to find the value of q.

Homework 2

Solve these equations.

1 $3(2x - 5) = 21$

2 $4(y + 3) = 3y + 7$

3 $3z - 2 = 2(z - 5)$

4 $2(3p + 1) = 4p + 3$

5 $3(q - 4) = 3 - 2q$

6 $5(2t - 7) = 25$

7 $8a - 1 = 2(a - 5)$

8 $2(2b - 9) = 2 + 3b$

9 $2 + 5c = 2(c - 2)$

10 $13d - 5 = 3(3d + 7)$

11 $6(1 - e) = 1 - 4e$

12 $12 - f = 3(4 - f)$

13 $3(7 + 3x) - 25 = 2x + 3$

14 $2(y - 9) + 3(y - 4) = 5$

15 $10 - 2(z + 5) = 8 - 3z$

16 $14 = 5 - 3(2t - 1)$

17 $3(3p - 2) - 4(p + 3) = 7$

18 $3(2q - 7) - (3q - 8) + 22 = 0$

19 Meena thinks of a number, adds 2 and then trebles the result.

Her answer is 36.

Write this as an equation.

Solve the equation to find Meena's number.

20 Jake thinks of a number, subtracts 5 and then multiplies the result by 4.

His answer is 52.

Write this as an equation.

Solve the equation to find Jake's number.

21 The side of the square is $(4p - 3)$ cm.

The base of the isosceles triangle is $(3p - 2)$ cm and each of the other sides is $(5p + 4)$ cm.

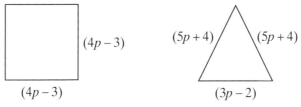

The perimeter of the square is equal to the perimeter of the triangle.

Use this information to write an equation.

Solve your equation to find the value of p.

22 In question **21**, what is the value of p if the base of the isosceles triangle is $(5p + 4)$ cm and the two sides are $(3p - 2)$ cm?

23 Jo is x years old. Jo's mother, Anne, is four times as old as Jo.

In four years' time, Anne will be three times as old as Jo.

Form an equation in x and solve it to find Jo's present age.

24 In one week, Ross worked 45 hours and was paid £302.10. His basic rate was £6.20 per hour and he worked x hours of overtime at £9.50 per hour.

Use this information to form an equation in x and solve it to find how many hours of overtime he worked.

Homework 3

Solve these equations.

1 $\dfrac{x}{5} - 2 = 1$

2 $\dfrac{y}{3} + 5 = 2$

3 $5 = 3 + \dfrac{z}{4}$

4 $7 = 4 - \dfrac{a}{3}$

5 $\dfrac{2b}{3} + 1 = 4$

6 $1 = 2 - \dfrac{5c}{6}$

7 $\dfrac{4x + 1}{3} = 7$

8 $\dfrac{3y - 5}{4} = 4$

9 $\dfrac{4z - 3}{5} = 3$

10 $\frac{1}{4}(2p + 7) = 1$

11 $\frac{1}{2}(3q + 1) = 5$

12 $\frac{1}{3}(4t - 9) = 6$

13 $\frac{1}{2}(3a - 1) = a - 5$

14 $\frac{1}{8}(2b - 3) = 3 - b$

15 $4c - 16 = \frac{1}{3}(8 - 2c)$

16 $\dfrac{x}{2} + \dfrac{x}{8} = 10$

17 $\dfrac{y}{3} - \dfrac{y}{12} = 7$

18 $\dfrac{5z}{6} - \dfrac{7z}{12} = 4$

19 $\dfrac{p}{6} = 5 - \dfrac{2p}{3}$

20 $\dfrac{3q}{4} - 5 = \dfrac{5q}{8}$

21 $\dfrac{3t}{4} - \dfrac{t}{3} = 7 - \dfrac{t}{6}$

22 Dylan says the answer to the equation $\dfrac{x + 4}{5} = 8 - x$ is $x = -9$.

Use substitution to check whether Dylan is correct.

23 Kamala and Jo are solving the equation $\dfrac{2y + 5}{4} = y - 1$.

Kamala gets the answer $y = 2.5$ and Jo gets $y = 4.5$
Check their answers to see if either of them is correct.

Homework 4 ▨

Solve these equations.

1 $\dfrac{2x-3}{3} + \dfrac{x-1}{6} = 3$

2 $\dfrac{y-4}{4} + \dfrac{y-5}{8} = 1$

3 $\dfrac{2z+11}{12} + \dfrac{z+6}{4} = 2$

4 $\dfrac{d-2}{3} - \dfrac{d+6}{7} = 0$

5 $\dfrac{2e+4}{9} - \dfrac{5-2e}{3} = 5$

6 $\dfrac{5f-3}{8} - \dfrac{f+2}{5} = \dfrac{1}{2}$

7 $\dfrac{x+4}{10} + \dfrac{2x+3}{2} = \dfrac{x+5}{5}$

8 $\dfrac{2y-1}{2} - \dfrac{y+9}{8} = \dfrac{y+1}{4}$

9 $\dfrac{z-2}{3} - \dfrac{z-3}{9} = \dfrac{z+6}{18}$

10 $\dfrac{3t+26}{20} - \dfrac{t+6}{5} = \dfrac{2t+7}{4}$

18 Reflections and rotations

Homework 1

1 a i Copy the diagram onto squared paper.

   ii Reflect A in the *x*-axis, and label its image P.

   iii Reflect B in the *x*-axis and label its image Q.

   b Repeat part **a** on new axes, but now reflect each shape in the *y*-axis.

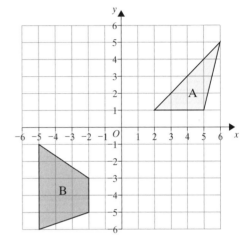

2 Draw a grid with the *x* and *y* axes labelled from −8 to 8.

   a Draw a parallelogram, P, with vertices at (0, 3), (3, 0), (3, 4) and (0, 7).

   b Draw the reflection of P in the line *x* = 4 and label it Q.

   c Draw the reflection of P in the line *x* = −2 and label it R.

3 Draw a grid with the *x* and *y* axes labelled from −6 to 6.

   a Draw triangle A by joining (−3, −2), (4, 0) and (2, 2).

   b Draw the reflection of A in the line *y* = 2. Label it B.

   c Draw the reflection of A in the line *y* = −2. Label it C.

4 When Sam was asked to reflect shape A in the line *y* = 2, he drew this diagram.

   a What did he do wrong?

   b Draw a diagram to show the correct image.

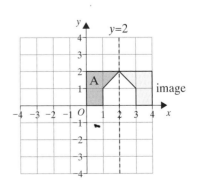

5 Get Real!

Many patterns on tiles are formed by reflecting shapes.

This diagram shows half of a tile.

Copy this onto squared paper and reflect the shapes in the line AB to show the rest of the pattern.

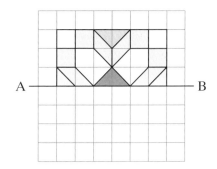

6 **a** Draw the mirror line $y = x$ on axes of x and y from −8 to 8.

   b Draw pentagon P with vertices at (1, 4), (4, 4), (4, 6), (2, 7) and (1, 6) and its image, Q, after reflection in the line $y = x$

   c Draw triangle T with vertices at (2, −2), (−2, −4) and (4, −4) and its image, U, after reflection in the line $y = x$

7 For this question draw a grid with the x- and y-axes labelled from −8 to 8.

   a Draw:

      i triangle A by joining (3, −3), (7, 1) and (8, −4)

      ii quadrilateral Q by joining (−3, 7), (2, 7), (3, 5) and (1, 2).

   b Draw the image of each shape after reflection in the line $y = -x$

   c Each shape and its image are congruent.

   Mark the sides and angles to show which are equal to each other.

8 **a** Copy the diagram onto squared paper.

   b Draw the image of the Z-shape after a rotation of 90° anticlockwise about the origin O. Label it A.

   c Draw the image of the Z-shape after a rotation of 180° about the origin O. Label it B.

   d Draw the image of the Z-shape after a rotation of 90° clockwise about the origin O. Label it C.

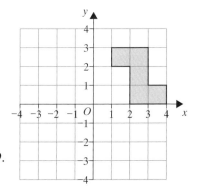

9 **a** On a grid with the x- and y- axes labelled from −6 to 6, draw parallelogram P by joining (0, −2), (4, −2), (6, −4) and (2, −4).

   b Draw the image of P after a quarter turn rotation clockwise about O and label the image Q.

10 **a** On a grid with the *x*- and *y*-axes labelled from −6 to 6, draw triangle T with vertices (−4, 2), (0, 2) and (−1, 5).

b Draw the image of T after a rotation of 90° clockwise about *O* and label the image U.

c Mark the corresponding sides and angles of T and U.

11 Meera says that when point (−2, 4) is rotated 90° anticlockwise about the origin the image point is (2, −4). Draw a sketch and say whether or not Meera is right.

12 Copy each shape onto isometric paper and show its image after the rotation described.

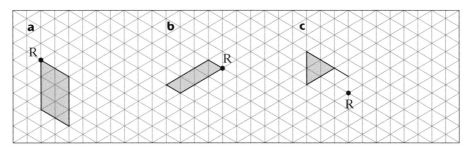

a Rotate through 60° anticlockwise about R.   **b** Rotate through 120° anticlockwise about R.   **c** Rotate through $\frac{1}{3}$ of a turn clockwise about R.

13 On squared paper draw a grid with the *x*- and *y*-axes labelled from −8 to 8.

a Draw and label trapezium T with vertices (3, 4), (5, 4), (6, 6) and (0, 6).

b Draw the image of T after a half turn about the point A(0, 4) and label it U.

c Draw the image of T after a half turn about the point B(0, −1) and label it V.

d Draw the image of T after a half turn about the point C(4, −1) and label it W.

e What do you notice about the three images?

14 On squared paper draw a grid with the *x*- and *y*-axes labelled from −6 to 6.

   a Join the points (2, −2), (3, −6) and (6, −6) to form a triangle and label it A.

   b Draw the image of A after a rotation of 90° clockwise about (2, −2). Label it B.

   c Draw the image of A after a rotation of 90° clockwise about the point (5, 1). Label it C.

   d Mark the sides and angles in A, B and C to show which are equal.

   e What can you say about the images?

15 **a** On a grid with the *x*- and *y*-axes labelled from −8 to 8 draw the quadrilateral, Q, with vertices at (−6, −4), (−3, −4), (−3, 0) and (−5, 1).

   b Draw the image of Q after a quarter turn anticlockwise about (−5, 1). Label it R.

   c Draw the image of Q after a quarter turn anticlockwise about (−2, −2). Label it S.

   d Draw the image of Q after a quarter turn anticlockwise about (−5, 4). Label it T.

Homework 2

1 Find the mirror line of the reflection that maps:

   a A onto B

   b A onto C

   c C onto D

   d B onto E

   e D onto H

   f E onto F

   g G onto K

   h F onto I

   i G onto E

   j J onto I

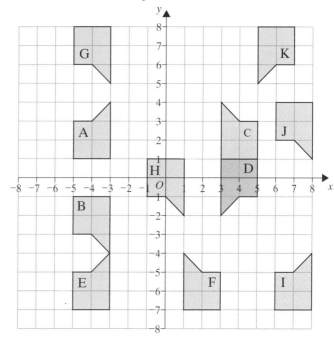

2 a On axes of x and y from −8 to 8 draw and label triangle A with vertices (−3, 6), (−3, 4) and (0, 4).

   b i Draw and label triangle B with vertices (−6, 3), (−4, 3) and (−4, 0).

     ii Describe fully the transformation that maps A onto B.

   c i Draw and label triangle C with vertices (6, −3), (4, −3) and (4, 0).

     ii Describe fully the transformation that maps A onto C.

   d Describe fully the transformation that maps B onto C.

3 Describe fully the rotation that maps:

   a A onto B

   b A onto C

   c A onto D

   d D onto E

   e B onto D

   f A onto F

   g C onto G

   h F onto H

   i B onto E

   j C onto D

   k H onto A

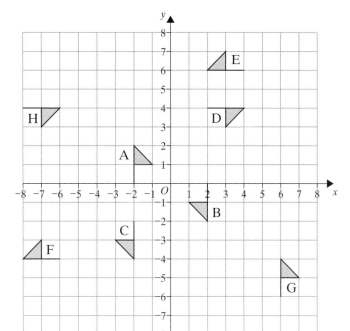

4 The diagram shows a quadrilateral ABCD and its image PQRS after a transformation.

   a Give a full description of the transformation.

   b Find and name the length that is equal to:

     i AB   **ii** CD   **iii** BD   **iv** AC

   c Find and name the angle that is equal to:

     i ∠CDA   **ii** ∠CAD   **iii** ∠AOB

   d Find and name a triangle that is congruent to:

     i DAB   **ii** CAD

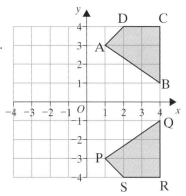

5 Describe fully the transformation that maps:

a A onto B

b B onto C

c A onto D

d C onto D

e A onto C

f D onto B

g C onto B

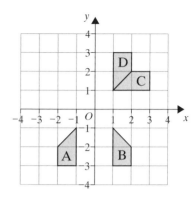

6 The diagram shows a trapezium ABCD and its image PQRS after a transformation.

a Give a full description of the transformation.

b Find and name the length that is equal to:

   i PQ   **iii** PS

   ii RS   **iv** PR

c Find and name the angle that is equal to:

   i ∠RSP   **iii** ∠PRS

   ii ∠RQP   **iv** ∠POS

d Find and name a triangle that is congruent to:

   i PQR   **iii** POS

   ii QPS

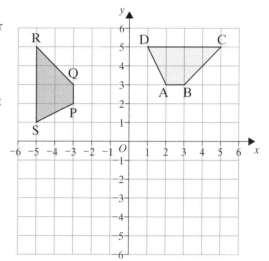

7 Get Real!

a Describe fully the transformation that maps the minute hand on a clock from its position at twelve o'clock to its position at twenty past twelve.

b Describe fully the transformation that maps the hour hand on a clock from its position at six o'clock to its position at half past eight.

8 **a** On axes of x and y from −6 to 6 draw rhombus R with vertices (4, 2), (5, 4), (4, 6) and (3, 4).

    b i Draw and label rhombus S with vertices (−4, 2), (−3, 4), (−4, 6) and (−5, 4).

      ii Find as many transformations as you can that map R onto S.
Describe each transformation fully.

    c i Draw and label rhombus T with vertices (−4, −2), (−5, −4), (−4, −6) and (−3, −4).

      ii Find as many transformations as you can that map R onto T.
Describe each transformation fully.

    d Find as many transformations as you can that map T onto S.
Describe each transformation fully.

9 On a grid with the x- and y-axes labelled from −8 to 8, draw these three pentagons.

        A(4, 1), B(7, 1), C(8, 4), D(6, 5), E(4, 3)

        P(1, 4), Q(3, 4), R(5, 6), S(4, 8), T(1, 7)

  and   J(1, −7), K(4, −8), L(5, −6), M(3, −4), N(1, −4)

    a Find and name two line segments that are equal in length to:

      i   AB   **ii** BC   **iii** AC

    b Describe fully the transformation that maps ABCDE onto PTSRQ.

    c Describe fully the transformation that maps ABCDE onto NJKLM.

    d Find and name two triangles that are congruent to:

      i   ABE   **ii** AED   **iii** OAE

10 PQRS and WXYZ are congruent squares.

They intersect at A, B, C, D, E, F, G and H and these points are the vertices of a regular octagon with centre O.

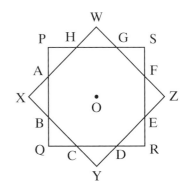

Describe fully the transformation that maps PQRS onto WXYZ in which

    a P is mapped onto W, Q onto X, R onto Y and S onto Z

    b P is mapped onto X, Q onto Y, R onto Z and S onto W

    c P is mapped onto W, Q onto Z, R onto Y and S onto X.

    d P is mapped onto Z, Q onto Y, R onto X and S onto W.

Homework 3

1 **a** Using a grid with the *x*- and *y*-axes labelled from −6 to 6, draw and label triangle T with vertices (−4, 5), (−2, 5) and (−4, 2).

  b Draw the reflection of triangle T in the *y*-axis and label it U.

  c Now draw the reflection of U in the *x*-axis and label it V.

  d Describe fully the single transformation that would map triangle T onto V.

2 **a** Using a grid with the *x*- and *y*-axes labelled from −6 to 6, draw trapezium A with vertices at (3, 4), (4, 4), (6, 2) and (2, 2).

  b Rotate A through 180° about *O* and label the image B.

  c Now reflect B in the *x*-axis and label the image C.

  d Describe fully the single transformation that would map A onto C.

3 **a** Using a grid with the *x*- and *y*-axes labelled from −6 to 6, draw kite K by joining (3, 5), (2, 4), (3, 1) and (4, 4).

  b Rotate K through 90° clockwise about *O* and label the image L.

  c Now draw the reflection of L in the *y*-axis and label it M.

  d Describe fully the single transformation that would map K onto M with point (2, 4) moving to point (−4, −2).

4 Draw a grid with the *x*- and *y*-axes labelled from −8 to 8.

  a Draw pentagon P with vertices at (1, 4), (4, 4), (4, 7), (3, 8) and (1, 7).

  b Draw the reflection of P in the line *y* = *x* and label the image R.

  c Now draw the reflection of R in the *x*-axis and label it S.

  d Describe fully the single transformation that would map P onto S.

<u>5</u> Draw a grid with the *x*- and *y*-axes labelled from −6 to 6.

  a Join the points (0, 3), (5, 4), (4, 1) and (2, 1) to give a quadrilateral, A.

  b **i** Rotate A through 180° about (3, 0) and label the image B.

    ii Mark the sides and angles in A and B to show which are equal.

  c **i** Now rotate B through 90° anticlockwise about (−2, −2) and label the image C.

    ii Mark the sides and angles in C to show which are equal to those in A and B.

  d Describe fully the single transformation that would map A onto C.

6 Draw a grid with the x- and y-axes labelled from -8 to 8.

   a Draw the triangle, P, with vertices at $(1, -3)$, $(3, -6)$ and $(6, -6)$.

   b i Rotate P through $90°$ anticlockwise about $(-1, 1)$ to give triangle Q.

     ii Mark the corresponding sides and angles in P and Q.

   c i Now reflect Q in $y = 1$ to give triangle R.

     ii Mark the corresponding sides and angles in R and P.

   d Describe fully the single transformation that would map P onto R.

7 On squared paper draw a grid with the x- and y-axes labelled from -8 to 8.

   a Draw a parallelogram by joining $A(1, 6)$, $B(4, 6)$, $C(2, 4)$ and $D(-1, 4)$.

   b Draw the reflection of ABCD in the line $y = x$ and label the image $A_1 B_1 C_1 D_1$ where A_1 is the image of A, B_1 is the image of B and so on.

   c Now draw the reflection of $A_1 B_1 C_1 D_1$ in the line $y = -x$ and label it $A_2 B_2 C_2 D_2$ where A_2 is the image of A_1, B_2 is the image of B_1 and so on.

   d Describe fully the single transformation that would map ABCD onto $A_2 B_2 C_2 D_2$ with A mapped to A_2, B to B_2 etc.

   e Describe in words another way of moving ABCD onto $A_2 B_2 C_2 D_2$ but in which A would not move to A_2.

8 What single transformation is equivalent to reflection in $y = x$ followed by reflection in $y = 2$?

Draw a diagram to illustrate your answer.

9 Sufia says, 'If you reflect a shape in $y = x$ and then rotate it $90°$ anticlockwise about O, you always get the same image that you would get if you rotated it $90°$ anticlockwise about O then reflected it in $y = x$.'

Is this statement true? Draw a diagram to illustrate your answer.

10 Use isometric dotty paper for this question.

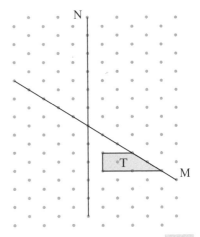

   a Draw two lines M and N at an angle of $60°$ and a trapezium, T, as shown.

   b Reflect T in M, then N.

   c Give a full description of the single transformation that would have the same effect on the trapezium.

   d What happens if you reflect T in N, then M?

Homework 4

1 Which of these 3-D solids have reflection symmetry?

In each case say how many different ways you can cut the shape into matching halves.

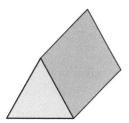

Triangular prism
(equilateral)

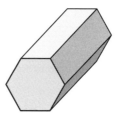

Hexagonal prism
(regular)

Hemisphere

2 **Get Real!**

How many planes of symmetry are there in each of these objects?

a Casserole dish   **b** Rolling pin   **c** Button   **d** Dart
                                                (back same
                                                 as front)

3 The following solids are made from cubes.

How many planes of symmetry does each solid have?

a   **b** 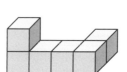   **c**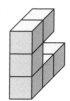

4 Each sketch below shows half of a solid made from cubes and a plane of symmetry.

Copy and complete each shape.

a 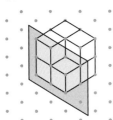   **b**

5 Sketch a prism whose cross-section is a regular pentagon.

How many planes of symmetry does this shape have?

6 Use an isometric grid.

  a Draw a 3-D shape that has two planes of symmetry.

  b Redraw your shape, but change it slightly so that it has just one plane of symmetry.

19 Ratio and proportion

 1 Simplify these ratios.

a	$3:6$	**e**	$3:18$	**i**	$25:35$	**m**	$0.6:0.4$
b	$3:9$	**f**	$3:21$	**j**	$75:100$	**n**	$3\frac{1}{2}:10\frac{1}{2}$
c	$3:12$	**g**	$14:28$	**k**	$\frac{3}{4}:\frac{5}{6}$	**o**	$25\%:75\%$
d	$3:15$	**h**	$9:36$	**l**	$2.5:3.5$	**p**	$75:200$

 2 **a** Write down three different pairs of numbers that are in the ratio $3:1$.

   b Write down three different pairs of numbers that are in the ratio $5:1$.

   c Explain how to find pairs of numbers that are in the ratio $5:1$.

   d Harry writes the three pairs of numbers 16 and 20, 14 and 18, and 12 and 16. He says these pairs of numbers are all in the same ratio. Is Harry correct? Explain your answer.

 3 **Get Real!**
Ben's GCSE results are D, A, B, C, C, E, D, B and C.

What is the ratio of Ben's number of Grade C and above results to his number of below grade C results?

 4 **Get Real!**
In a large college, staffing costs are £15 million and other costs are £5 million. Find the ratio of staffing costs : other costs in its simplest form.

5 Get Real!

A recipe lists the following quantities of ingredients to make six scones.

Self-raising flour	240 grams
Salt	0.5 teaspoon
Sultanas	75 grams
Butter	40 grams
Caster sugar	25 grams
Egg	1 large
Milk	20 mℓ

a List the ingredients needed for 12 scones.

b How much flour would be needed for 15 scones?

6 Get Real!

In a nursery, the number of children is 24 and the number of nurses is 4.

a What is the nurse : child ratio?

b Using this ratio, find how many nurses are needed for 30 children.

7 Get Real!

Red and yellow paint are mixed in the ratio 2 : 5 to make the colour 'Hot Orange'.

a Which of these mixes will make 'Hot Orange' paint?

Amount of red paint (litres)	Amount of yellow paint (litres)
2	5
3	6
3	4
5	2
4	10
6	15
1	$2\frac{1}{2}$

b Write down another possible pair of amounts of red and yellow paint that would make 'Hot Orange'.

c Would it make any difference if the amounts were measured in pints instead of litres? Give a reason for your answer.

8 Get Real!

The aspect ratio of a film is the ratio of the width of the picture to its height. A common Cinemascope aspect ratio is 2.35 : 1.

Using this aspect ratio, find:

a the width of a picture if its height is 2 metres

b the height of a picture whose width is 4 metres.

9 The ratio $x:y$ simplifies to 2 : 9.

a If x is 6, what is y?

b If y is 36, what is x?

c If y is 13.5, what is x?

d If x and y add up to 55, what are x and y?

10 Make up another question like question **9** and give the answers.

 **11 Get Real!**

a Find, in their simplest forms, the teacher : student ratios for these schools.

School	Number of teachers	Number of students
School 1	63	945
School 2	16	280
School 3	27	567
School 4	125	2275
School 5	55	880

b i If a school with 40 teachers had the same teacher : student ratio as School 1, how many students would it have?

ii If a school with 1500 students had the same teacher : student ratio as School 1, how many teachers would it have?

Homework 2

 1 Divide these numbers and quantities in the ratio 1 : 4.

a 200   **c** £6.50   **e** £2.50

b 350   **d** 8 litres   **f** 3.5 litres

 2 Divide the numbers and quantities in question **1** in the ratio 2 : 3.

3 Divide the numbers and quantities in question **1** in the ratio 7 : 3.

4 Divide the numbers and quantities in question **1** in the ratio 1 : 4 : 5.

5 Get Real!

Salad dressing is made from oil and vinegar in the ratio 3 : 1.

  a How much oil is needed to make 100 ml of salad dressing?

  b How much vinegar is needed to make 0.4 litres of salad dressing?

  c How much salad dressing can you make if you have plenty of oil but only 20 ml of vinegar?

6 **a** Find the number of boys and the number of girls in these schools.

School	Total number of students	Boy : girl ratio
School A	2000	1 : 1
School B	1800	2 : 7
School C	1860	2 : 3
School D	525	8 : 7
School E	1055	100 : 111

  b Find the boy : girl ratios in part **a** in the form $1 : n$ (in other words, find how many girls there are for every boy).

  c Which school has the largest proportion of girls? Give a reason for your answer.

7 **a** Work out the amount of protein in 100 g of each of these foods.

Food	Carbohydrate : fat : protein ratio
Fudge biscuits	9 : 2 : 1
Strawberries	11 : 1 : 1
Scambled eggs	1 : 2 : 2
Chilli con carne	7 : 6 : 7
Italian sausage	1 : 5 : 4

  b How many grams of chilli con carne do you need to eat to have 100 g of protein?

  c How many grams of fudge biscuits do you need to eat to have 100 g of protein?

8 A school has £10 000 to spend on ICT equipment. The amount is to be split between the lower school and the upper school in the ratio of the number of students. There are 545 students in the lower school and 495 in the upper school.

How much money does each part of the school have to spend?

 9 Pen metal for pen nibs is an alloy of copper, gold and silver in the ratio $2:1:1$.

a How much of each metal is needed to make 1 kilogram of pen metal?

b If there are only 145 grams of gold left but plenty of copper and silver, how much pen metal can be made?

c How much gold would there be in a pen nib weighing 2 grams?

Homework 3

1 Get Real!

Jane pays £2.40 for 8 pencils.

How much would 20 of the same pencils cost?

2 Get Real!

Ali worked for 6 hours one day and earned £105.60

a How much will he be paid for a day when he works for 8 hours at the same rate of pay?

b Complete a copy of this table. Plot the values in the table as points on a graph, using the numbers of hours worked as the x-coordinates and the money earned as the corresponding y-coordinates.

Number of hours worked	0	2	4	6	8	10
Money earned (£)				105.60		

c The points should lie in a straight line through $(0, 0)$.

i Explain why.

ii What does the gradient of the line represent?

iii Show how to use the graph to find out how long Ali has to work to earn £100.

3 Get Real!

To make sandwiches for 3 people on 5 days, 750 g of meat is needed.

a How much meat is needed for sandwiches for 8 people on 1 day?

b How many days' sandwiches for 4 people will 600 g of meat make?

c Sandwiches for 5 people for 4 days needs the same amount of meat as sandwiches for 10 days for how many people?

4 Get Real!

Softouch hand cream is packed in small and large sizes, as shown in the table:

	Amount of hand cream	Price
Small size	55 grams	£1.05
Large size	225 grams	£4.35

Which size is better value for money?

Show how you worked out your answer.

5 Get Real!

A journey of 240 kilometres took 5 hours.

a How far would you go in 4 hours at the same average speed?

b How far would you go in three quarters of an hour at this average speed?

c How long would it take to travel 400 kilometres at this average speed?

6 Get Real!

A mail order company offers to supply and deliver boxes of

22 chocolates for £17.95

44 chocolates for £27.95

66 chocolates for £35.95.

a Which of these is the best value for money? Show how you worked it out.

b Write a sentence suggesting why there is such a difference in the price per chocolate.

7 Get Real!

Notice that the two parts of this question are really the same! Use part **a** to help you work out part **b**

a 75% of a number is 6. Use the unitary method to find 100% of the number.

b A T-shirt is £6 with the special offer (25% off).
What was the original price of the T-shirt?

8 **a** Two numbers are in the ratio 1 : 0.6

The first number is 15; what is the second?

b Two numbers are in the ratio 1 : 0.6

The second number is 12; what is the first?

c Three numbers are in the ratio 1.2 : 1 : 0.8

The third number is 36; what are the other two numbers?

9 Get Real!

The weights of objects on other planets are proportional to their weights on Earth. A person weighing 150 pounds on Earth would weigh 60 pounds on Mercury and 160 pounds on Saturn.

a What would a person weighing 100 pounds on Earth weigh on Mercury?

b What would a mineral sample weighing 20 kilograms on Saturn weigh on Earth?

c Sketch a graph to show the weights of objects on Mercury compared with their weights on Earth.

d Express the ratio 'weight of object on Earth : weight of object on Mercury : weight of object on Saturn' as simply as you can.

Homework 4

1 At the beginning of 2000, Jack invested £740 in a savings account, which paid interest at an annual rate of 3.5%, and was added on to the account in December each year.

How much did Jack have in the account at the end of:

a 2000

b 2005?

c How much interest has Jack's money earned between the beginning of 2000 and the end of 2005?

Round your answers sensibly when necessary.

2 Angela's annual salary is £21 000. She expects to be given a rise of 1.8% of her salary every year.

a What will Angela's salary be after 2 years?

b What difference would it make to Angela's salary after 2 years if she were given a rise of 0.9% every six months instead of 1.8% a year?

3 Anne's savings in a building society account increase from £3400 to £3515.60 in one year.

a What annual rate of interest is paid on Anne's account?

b How much money will Anne have after 5 years if the building society continues to pay interest at this rate?

c Anne wants her savings to exceed £5000. After how many years will this happen?

4 A population of bacteria is increasing in size by 5% every hour. There are 500 bacteria to begin with.

Find, to the nearest 10, the number of bacteria after:

a 2 hours

b one and a half hours

c 50 minutes

d one day.

5 The mass of cells in a laboratory cell culture is doubling every 24 hours. At the start of the experiment, the mass of the cells is 25 grams.

a Find the mass of the cells after:

i 2 days

ii a week

iii 12 hours.

b By how much is the mass of the cells multiplied after 12 hours?

c Assuming the same growth rate, what was the mass of the cells 24 hours before the experiment started?

d Write down a formula for the mass of the cells t days from the start of the experiment.

6 House prices are increasing at 5% a year.

a What will be the price of a house costing £78 000 now in 2 years' time?

b What would a house costing £100 000 now have been worth last year?

c How realistic do you think it is to say that house prices go up by 5% a year?

7 John puts £100 into a savings account to which 2.5% interest is added every six months.

a How much will John have in his account at the end of 1 year?

b If instead, 5% interest had been added at the end of the year how much would be in his account?

c After 3 years, how much more interest has John earned with 2.5% interest added twice a year than with 5% interest added once a year?

8 From the age of 2 years to the age of 5 years, the value of a car depreciates by 20% each year. Its value when it is 2 years old is £6500.

  a What will the car be worth when it is 3 years old?

  b What will the car be worth when it is 5 years old?

9 The radioactive isotope, Chromium 51, decays at such a rate that it loses half its mass every month.

  a What will be the mass of 10 kg of Chromium 51 after a year?

  b Estimate what percentage of its mass Chromium 51 loses each day. (Assume a month is 30 days.)

10 The radioactive isotope of carbon, Carbon 14, is used in carbon dating of ancient objects. The half-life of Carbon 14 is approximately 5700 years (that is, it takes 5700 years for any mass of Carbon 14 to decrease to half that mass).

  Sketch a graph to show how the mass of Carbon 14 decreases over many years.

Homework 5

1 y is proportional to the square of x (that is, $y = kx^2$) and when $x = 1$, $y = 4$.

  a Find the value of the constant k.

  b Find y when $x = 2$.

2 y is proportional to the square of x, and when $x = 5$, $y = 25$.

  a Write an equation showing the relationship between x and y.

  b Find the value of the constant in your equation.

  c Find x when:

  i $y = 64$ **ii** $y = 60$

3 Get Real!

The cost, £C, of a railway journey is directly proportional to the distance travelled, d miles.

A 20-mile journey costs £3.20

  a Find an equation connecting C and d.

  b Use your equation to find

  i the cost of a 105-mile journey

  ii the length of a journey costing £100.

4   Get Real!

The time, t hours, taken for a journey of a fixed length is inversely proportional to the average speed, v m.p.h., of the journey. When the average speed is 45 m.p.h., the time taken is 3 hours.

a Find how long the journey takes at an average speed of 40 m.p.h.

b Find the speed necessary to complete the journey in two and a half hours.

5   Get Real!

The number of days, d, needed to complete a business project is inversely proportional to the number of people, n, working on the project. It will take 10 people 3 days to do the work.

a Find an equation connecting d and n.

b How long will 5 people take to complete the project?

c How many people are needed to complete the project in 2 days?

d Sketch a graph of d against n.

6 Two variables, p and q, are such that p is directly proportional to q.

Which of the following statements are true?

a If q is doubled, p is halved.

b The graph of p against q is a straight line through the origin.

c q is inversely proportional to p.

d p and q satisfy an equation of the form $p = kq$.

7 One litre is equal to one and three quarter pints.

a Write a formula to find the number of litres, L, that are equivalent to P pints.

b Use your formula to draw a conversion graph for pints and litres and use the graph to convert 10 pints to litres.

c Write a sentence to show the proportional relationship between litres and pints.

8 Say what sort of proportion (direct proportion, inverse proportion or neither) exists between these variables.

a Circumference of circle and diameter.

b Time taken to complete a task and number of people available to do it.

c Area of square and square of its perimeter.

d Fahrenheit temperatures and corresponding Celsius temperatures.

e Number of weeks and the corresponding number of days.

f Number of glasses of water that can be poured from a bottle and the amount of water poured into each glass.

9 Write an algebraic statement for each of these relationships.

   a y is directly proportional to x.

   b The product of x and y is a constant.

   c y is proportional to the square of x.

   d y is inversely proportional to x.

   Sketch a graph for each one.

10 Could x be directly proportional to y in this table?
Give a reason for your answer.

x	1	5	9	13
y	1.8	8.8	15.8	22.8

11 The area of the surface of a sphere is proportional to the square of its radius. A sphere of radius 10 cm has a surface area of 1257 cm^2.

   a What is the surface area of a sphere with a radius of:

     i 5 cm

     ii 20 cm?

   b Sketch a graph of the relationship.

12 The masses of two similar shapes are proportional to the cubes of their lengths. The first shape has a mass of 50 g and a length of 10 cm. The second has a mass of 100 g. Find its length.

13 Most conversion graphs express directly proportional relationships.

   a Give an example of such a conversion graph.

   b The conversion between Fahrenheit and Celsius temperatures does not represent a relationship of direct proportion. Explain this statement, drawing a sketch graph to illustrate your explanation.